Shining Star

C

Workbook

Anna Uhl Chamot

Pam Hartmann

Jann Huizenga

with

Steve Sloan

Longman

longman.com

Shining Star ★c

Workbook

Pearson Education, 10 Bank Street, White Plains, NY 10606

Workbook consultant: Steve Sloan

Vice president, director of instructional design: Allen Ascher
Editorial director: Ed Lamprich
Acquisitions editor: Amanda Rappaport Dobbins
Project manager: Susan Saslow
Workbook manager: Donna Schaffer
Senior development editor: Lauren Weidenman
Vice president, director of design and production: Rhea Banker
Executive managing editor: Linda Moser
Production manager: Ray Keating
Senior production editor: Sylvia Dare
Director of manufacturing: Patrice Fraccio
Senior manufacturing buyer: Edith Pullman
Photo research: Kirchoff/Wohlberg, Inc.
Design and production: Kirchoff/Wohlberg, Inc.
Cover design: Rhea Banker, Tara Mayer
Text font: 11/14 Franklin Gothic
Acknowledgments: See page 169
Illustrations: 38 Tony Smith; 54, 55 John Hovell; 77 Tom Leonard; 95 Tom
    Leonard; 101, 108, 112 Philip Argent; 124 John Hovell.
Photos: 3, 10, 11 Dorling Kindersley; 12 Kevin Fleming/CORBIS; 18, 24, 25,
    39 Dorling Kindersley; 40, 52 Bettmann/CORBIS; 53 AP/Wide World
    Photos; 56 Xavier Bonghi/Getty Images; 60 AP/Wide World Photos;
    66 Morton Beebe/CORBIS; 73 Peter Gridley/Taxi/Getty Images; 96 CORBIS;
    98 Bettmann/CORBIS; 109, 111 Dorling Kindersley; 115 NASA; 122, 125
    Dorling Kindersley; 126 NASA; 130, 138, 139, 140 Dorling Kindersley;
    150 PhotoDisc/Getty Images; 151 Index Stock Imagery.

ISBN: 0-13-049968-4

Printed in the United States of America
        12 13 14 15–BAH–11 10 09

Welcome to *Shining Star's* Workbook. Exercises in each unit of this book will help you practice the skills and strategies you've already learned throughout the *Shining Star* program. You'll have fun completing crossword puzzles as you build your vocabulary. Other activities will help you apply reading strategies and practice language-development skills in grammar, spelling, writing, proofreading, and editing.

To help you get the most out of your *Shining Star* reading experiences, we've added an exciting feature—Reader's Companion. The Reader's Companion activities will help you better understand and explore the "Connect to Literature" and "Connect to Content" selections in your Student Book.

Reader's Companion begins with a summary that tells you what the selection is about before you read. Then a visual summary helps you focus on the main ideas and details, as well as the organization of each selection. Use What You Know lets you explore your own knowledge or experience before you read. You'll apply reading strategies that you've already learned, show that you know about the kind of selection you're reading—whether it's an informational text or a song. You'll check your comprehension or understanding of a selection and enjoy using literary elements. You'll find write-on-lines for recording your answers. Whenever you see the Mark the Text symbol, you'll know that you should underline, circle, or mark the text. We hope you enjoy choosing from the many creative activities designed to suit your own learning styles.

After reading, Reader's Companion will give you opportunities to retell selections in creative ways—using your own words. You can also write your thoughts and reactions to the selection. Then you can comment on how certain skills and strategies were helpful to you. Thinking about a skill will help you apply it to other reading situations.

We hope you'll enjoy showing what you know as you complete the many and varied activities included in your *Shining Star* Workbook.

CONTENTS

Copyright © 2004 by Pearson Education, Inc.

CONTENTS

CONTENTS

UNIT 1 Points of View

PART 1

Contents

VOCABULARY

Use with textbook page 5.

Read each sentence. Circle the letter for the best meaning of the underlined word.

1. The workers unloaded <u>cargo</u> from the ship.

    a. goods   b. battles   c. taxes   d. rides

2. The spy who sold secrets to the enemy country was a <u>traitor</u>.

    a. hero   b. fighter   c. coward   d. betrayer

3. The people wanted <u>independence</u> from the country that was ruling them.

    a. money   b. freedom   c. taxes   d. goods

4. The farmers couldn't sell their crops because of the people's <u>boycott</u>.

    a. disguise   b. promise   c. mistake   d. protest

5. The store owner couldn't pay his rent because he was having <u>financial</u> problems.

    a. health   b. money   c. sleeping   d. tax

Read the clues. Use the words in the box to complete the crossword puzzle. (Hint: You will not use all the words.)

pound	disguised	company	uproar	British
uproar	financial	cargo	traitor	protest

ACROSS

2. hid who they were
3. noise and confusion
5. one who turns against his country

DOWN

1. having to do with money
4. goods that are carried by ship or truck

Name _____ Date _____

Understanding Homographs

Homographs are words that are spelled the same but have different meanings. Homographs can have different pronunciations.

show/show	can/can
I will **show** you how to brew tea.	You **can** visit us in Boston this summer.
My sister has the starring role in the **show**.	I don't like food that comes in a **can**.

Circle the correct meaning of each underlined homograph.

Example: More than fifteen million <u>pounds</u> of tea sat in the warehouse.

(a. units of weight)   b. reduce to powder

1. He gave an <u>order</u> for his troops to leave immediately.

   a. command   b. organization

2. The colonists did not accept Parliament's <u>right</u> to tax them.

   a. opposite of wrong   b. something the law says you can do

3. I will <u>stuff</u> the bag with presents.

   a. a lot of things   b. fill something full

4. If we have <u>fair</u> weather tomorrow, we can have a picnic.

   a. good   b. a market where goods are sold

5. They had to pay a <u>fine</u> for parking in the wrong place.

   a. penalty   b. well

READING STRATEGY

Use with textbook page 5.

Previewing

Previewing a text helps you better understand what you read. When you preview, read the title and the headings. Then look at the pictures, maps, and illustrations. Read the first and last paragraph of each section. Think about what you already know about the subject and as you preview, ask: What do I know about the topic? What questions might be answered as I read?

In your textbook, preview pages 6 and 7 of "Moving Toward Independence: The Boston Tea Party."

1. What do you learn from reading the title of this article?

_____

_____

2. What is the heading on page 6? What does it tell you?

_____

_____

3. What do you learn from the first sentence in the paragraph on page 6? What questions do you think of when you read it?

_____

_____

4. Look at the pictures and captions on pages 6 and 7 in your textbook. What do they tell you about the text?

_____

_____

5. Use what you learned from the title, headings, illustrations, and what you read. What do you think you will learn in this article?

_____

_____

_____

_____

Use with textbook pages 14–16.

Summary: "Yankee Doodle" and "The World Turned Upside Down"

These songs are both associated with the American Revolution, the war in which American colonists won their independence from the British. People believe that American colonists sang "Yankee Doodle" to celebrate their victory over the British at Yorktown. "The World Turned Upside Down" describes a world where nothing makes sense. Some people think British soldiers sang this song after they surrendered at Yorktown.

Visual Summary

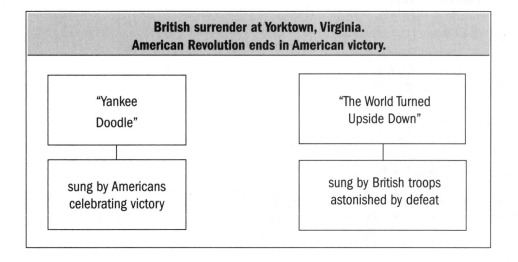

British surrender at Yorktown, Virginia.
American Revolution ends in American victory.

"Yankee Doodle"

"The World Turned Upside Down"

sung by Americans celebrating victory

sung by British troops astonished by defeat

Yankee Doodle

Father and I went down to camp,
Along with Captain Gooding,
And there we saw the men and boys
As thick as hasty pudding.

Chorus:
Yankee Doodle keep it up,
Yankee Doodle Dandy,
Mind the music and the step,
And with the girls be handy.

There was Captain Washington
Upon a slapping stallion,
Giving orders to his men,
I guess there was a million.

Repeat chorus.

_____

hasty pudding, thick, sweet, creamy food popular during colonial times
Yankee Doodle, originally used by the British to mean "American fool," but adopted by the Americans as a way to refer to themselves
mind, pay attention to
Captain, military title meaning "chief"

Important Events of the American Revolution

Study the timeline.

	1773	Boston Tea Party
	1774	
Paul Revere's ride	1775	Battle of Concord (April 19) Battle of Bunker Hill (June 17)
	1776	Declaration of Independence
	1777	American victory at Saratoga, turning point of war
France recognizes American independence.	1778	
Spain enters the war against Britain.	1779	
	1780	
British surrender at Yorktown.	1781	
	1782	
	1783	Britain recognizes American independence in the Treaty of Paris.

_____

victory, win
turning point, moment when things change

Text Structure: Timeline

This timeline shows important events in the American Revolution. Circle the final victory for the Americans. **MARK THE TEXT** How many years passed from the Battle of Concord, when the first shot of the Revolution was fired, until this final victory?

_____

Comprehension Check

Draw a box around the battle called the turning point of the **MARK THE TEXT** war and the note explaining what a turning point is. How do you think this battle was a turning point in the war?

_____

_____

_____

_____

_____

Reading Strategy: Using Background Knowledge

Underline the two countries that supported the American side and the treaty that ended **MARK THE TEXT** the war. Based on the treaty's name and your background knowledge, write the name of the country in which the treaty was signed.

_____

The World Turned Upside Down

If buttercups buzz'd after the bee,
If boats were on land, churches on sea,
If ponies rode men,
And if grass ate the cows,
And cats should be chased
Into holes by the mouse,
If the mamas sold their babies
To the gypsies for half a crown,
If summer were spring,
And the other way 'round,
Then all the world would be upside down.

_____

buttercups, small plants with bright yellow flowers shaped like cups
bee, black and yellow insect that makes honey, using pollen from
    flowers such as buttercups
gypsies, group of people usually living a nomadic life
half a crown, British coin (no longer in use)

Reading Strategy: Using Background Knowledge

Underline and number the first six conditions stated in the song. **MARK THE TEXT** Using what you know about the relationships described in the conditions, explain what they all have in common.

_____

_____

Comprehension Check

Draw two lines under the line that tells what the world would be like if the conditions **MARK THE TEXT** were met. Some believe the British sang this song about the victory of the untrained colonists. How does the view of the world expressed in the song relate to that event?

_____

_____

_____

Text Structure: Song

In many songs, words rhyme at the ends of lines. Rhyming words have the same ending sounds. For example, *dandy* and *handy* rhyme. Circle the words that rhyme at the ends of lines in this song, **MARK THE TEXT** and draw a line to connect each rhyming pair. What effect do the rhyming words have?

_____

_____

_____

Choose one and complete:
1. Draw a map to show where the different battles of the American Revolution were fought. Use an atlas or a map on the Internet to help you. Include all the battles shown on the timeline on page 7 of this workbook.
2. Choose one event on the timeline, and find out more about it by researching it in a history book or on the Internet. Explain why the event was important.
3. Listen to the two songs and then research one of them on the Internet or in other sources. Create your own audiocassette, videotape, or written report about the song, its different versions, and its history.

Retell It!

Imagine that you were a soldier in the Revolution singing one of these songs. Describe the situation and your feelings.

_____

_____

_____

_____

_____

Reader's Response

How did the songs help you appreciate the experiences of soldiers in the American Revolution or the experiences of soldiers in general?

_____

_____

_____

_____

_____

Think About the Skill

How did your background knowledge help you better understand the songs?

_____

_____

_____

_____

_____

_____

_____

_____

Name _____ Date _____

GRAMMAR

Use with textbook page 18.

The Simple Past
The **simple past** describes an action that happened in the past.

Rule	Present	Past
Add **-ed** to the base form of regular verbs.	warn protest	warned protested
Add **-d** to regular verbs that end with e.	refuse serve	refused served
Irregular verbs have special past forms.	sell pay	sold paid
For negative past sentences, use **did not (didn't)** + **verb**	does not accept does not like	did not accept did not like

Read the sentences below. Circle the regular past forms. Underline the irregular past forms.

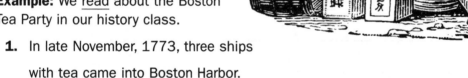

Example: We <u>read</u> about the Boston Tea Party in our history class.

1. In late November, 1773, three ships with tea came into Boston Harbor.

2. The Sons of Liberty wanted the ships to leave the harbor.

3. The Sons of Liberty asked the governor for aid.

4. The governor refused their request.

5. The governor ordered the ships to remain in the harbor.

Write the correct past tense form of the verb in parentheses ( ) on the lines.

6. The colonists (bolt) _____ out of the darkness and (jump)

    _____ onto the cargo ships.

7. They (shout) _____ as they (dump) _____ the tea
    into the harbor.

8. The tea chests (float) _____ in the water.

9. The dampness (ruin) _____ the tea.

10. The British did not (look) _____ happy.

Name _____ Date _____

GRAMMAR

Use after the lesson on present tense verbs.

Using the Present Tense

For **regular** English verbs, use the base form of the verb with *I, you, we,* and *they.* Add *-s* or *-es* to the base form of the verb when using *he, she,* or *it.*

Some verbs are **irregular**. You must learn these individually.

I am	we are
he is	you are
she is	they are
it is	

Complete the sentences using the simple present tense form of the verbs in parentheses ( ).

Example: She (love) _____ *loves* _____ to study.

1. We (study) _____ to learn about the past.

2. American history (be) _____ very interesting.

3. I (like)_____ Colonial history most of all.

4. The colonists (decide) _____ to boycott tea.

5. My teacher (show) _____ us a book with amazing pictures of the Boston Harbor.

Circle the correct verb.

Example: Colonists (⟨dress⟩/ dresses) as Mohawk Indians.

6. They (rush / rushes) into the meetinghouse.

7. Many people (follow / follows) them to the harbor.

8. A man (board / boards) one of the ships.

9. It (is / are) full of tea!

10. I (hate / hates) this part of the story.

SKILLS FOR WRITING

Use with textbook page 19.

Using Sequence Words in Narrative Writing

A **narrative text** usually tells a story about events in the past. The events are often presented in chronological order. Many writers use **sequence words** to show the order in which the events took place.

Complete the sentences. Use the sequence words above each group of sentences to show chronological order.

finally   first   next

1. _____, British placed a tax on tea.

2. _____, merchants sold tea at a higher price.

3. _____, the colonists began a tea boycott.

this morning   yesterday   last weekend

4. _____, I saw a movie about the Boston Tea Party.

5. _____, I bought a book with more facts about the event.

6. _____, I gave a report on the movie and book.

second   after that   first   last

7. _____, the colonists put on disguises.

8. The _____ thing they did was head for Boston Harbor.

9. Soon _____, they broke open the tea chests.

10. Their _____ act was to dump the tea into the water.

Unit 1 Points of View   Part 1

PROOFREADING AND EDITING

Use with textbook page 20.

Read the narrative carefully. Find all the mistakes. Then rewrite the narrative correctly on the lines below.

Learning About the American Revolution

Trevor needed to learn more about the American revolution. He had a paper due on Monday for his history class He only had three days left to write it.

On friday afternoon, he goed to the library and askd the librarian for help. he check out three books. After looking through the books, he decided to write about the Boston Tea Party Later in the day, he began taking notes about the historic event.

On saturday, he reviewd his notes. Then he start the first draft of her report. after two hours of writing, he was finished. On sunday morning, he read over the report and made a few changes. First, he wrote some notes on his first draft. Last, he writed his final draft. Finally, he reread the report. It was ready to turn in and he knowed it was well written!

_____

_____

_____

_____

_____

_____

_____

_____

_____

_____

_____

_____

SPELLING

Use after the lesson on spelling.

Spelling the Long and Short *a* and *i* Sounds

Here are some words with the short *a* and the short *i* vowel sounds. Note how the short vowel sounds are spelled.

| short *a* sound: | **tax   sat   fan   past** | spelled *a* |
| short *i* sound: | **visit,   with   mist   inn** | spelled *i* |

Some words have a long vowel sound. Here are some words with the long *a* and the long *i* sounds. Note how the long vowel sounds are spelled.

| long *a*: | **paid   day   late** | spelled **ai   ay,   a_e** |
| long *i*: | **twice   high   sky   hi   pie** | spelled **i_e   igh   y   i   ie** |

Circle the words with the short *a* sound and underline the words with the long *i* sound.

Example: (pat)   twist   see   <u>sly</u>

1. dry   tree   trap   lane

2. fame   sham   fry   fish

3. did   date   that   tie

4. slap   chip   slide   tame

5. bait   understand   flight   rim

Circle the words with the long *a* sound and underline the words with the short *i* sound.

6. plain   plan   pie   pick

7. simple   sample   stale   style

8. mail   mild   mill   matter

9. sight   standard   spray   silly

10. file   fill   fail   fancy

UNIT 1 Points of View

PART 2

Contents

VOCABULARY

Use with textbook page 23.

Read each sentence. Circle the letter for the word or phrase that means the same as the underlined word.

1. The new mother showed warmth and <u>affection</u> for her baby.

a. love   b. pictures   c. blankets   d. messages

2. In the United States, people <u>customarily</u> shake hands when they meet someone.

a. oddly   b. usually   c. sometimes   d. strangely

3. People who speak Chinese and English can <u>translate</u> stories into English.

a. sing   b. change   c. sing   d. remember

4. The citizens were <u>scandalized</u> by the politician's bad behavior.

a. interested   b. pleased   c. thrilled   d. outraged

5. The <u>witness</u> to the car wreck told the police what she saw.

a. observer   b. official   c. villager   d. respect

Read the clues. Use the words in the box to complete the crossword puzzle. (Hint: You will not use all the words.)

scandalized	husband	dialect	affection
witness	English	remembers	translate

ACROSS

3. the way a language is spoken by a particular group of people

5. caring and tenderness

DOWN

1. person who sees something occur

2. very upset by something

4. change into another language

VOCABULARY BUILDING

Understanding Prefixes

Many words begin with a **prefix**. Adding a prefix to a base word changes the meaning of that word. Knowing the meaning of a prefix and the meaning of a base word can help you define words with prefixes. The prefix **un-** means "not." Adding this prefix to a word makes the word mean the opposite. Here are two examples from *Daughter of China*.

Prefix	Base Word	Prefix + Base Word	Meaning
un-	afraid	unafraid	not afraid
un-	comfortable	uncomfortable	not comfortable

Look at each word with a prefix. Write the meaning of the word.

Example: unhappy: _____*not happy*_____

1. unknown: _____

2. unlike: _____

3. unlocked: _____

4. unbelievable: _____

5. unfair: _____

The prefixes **im-** and **in-** also mean "**not.**"
    im- + proper = improper   in- + just = injust

Make new words by adding the prefix to the base word. Write the meaning of the new word.

	New Word	**Definition**
6. un- + decided:	_____	_____
7. un- + able:	_____	_____
8. im- + possible:	_____	_____
9. in- + complete:	_____	_____
10. un- + popular:	_____	_____

READING STRATEGY

Use with textbook page 23.

Using Knowledge and Experience to Predict

Previewing a text helps you predict what it will be about. As you preview, use what you already know to help you predict what the text may be about. Ask yourself these questions:

- When and where does the selection take place?
- What do I know about this time and place?
- What can I guess about the people and their lives?
- What is my purpose for reading this text?

This information will help you predict what might happen in the text.

Preview pages 24–29 of *Daughter of China* in your textbook. Notice the two parts of the selection. Then answer the questions.

1. When and where do the events take place?

_____

2. Who do you think is telling this narrative? Who are the other people in it?

_____

_____

3. What kinds of problems do you think the narrator and the others she writes about will face?

_____

_____

4. Have you ever been in similar situations? Explain one.

_____

_____

5. What is your purpose for reading this narrative?

_____

_____

_____

_____

_____

Use with textbook pages 32–34.

Summary: "Understanding Cultural Differences"

Every culture has its own way of saying and doing things. A word or action that means one thing in one culture may mean something else in another. This pamphlet gives advice to people who attend or work at a camp whose campers and staff members come from different cultural backgrounds. The pamphlet offers tips for improving communication and avoiding misunderstanding. It also encourages campers and staff members to learn about and respect other cultures.

Visual Summary

Tips for Understanding Cultural Differences
• A smile shows pleasure or happiness in some cultures but confusion, embarrassment, disagreement, anger, or frustration in others.
• Eye contact is respectful in some cultures, disrespectful in others.
• In some cultures, people are told never to say "no" and so may say "yes" when they don't really mean it.
• In some cultures, people use first names soon after meeting; in others, people do not.
• People from different cultures have different views of what it means to be on time, late, or early.

Use What You Know

List three things that can make talking with people from other cultures difficult.

1. _____

2. _____

3. _____

Text Structure: Informational Pamphlet

An informational pamphlet is a printed handout giving useful information to readers. Underline the words in the first paragraph that explain the purpose of this pamphlet. Who will read the pamphlet?

MARK THE TEXT

_____

_____

Reading Strategy: Monitoring Comprehension

When you monitor comprehension, you make sure you understand what you are reading. One way to monitor comprehension is to ask yourself questions about key terms or topics and then try to answer them. Circle a key term or topic in the second paragraph on this page. Ask and answer a question about the term or topic you circled.

MARK THE TEXT

_____

_____

_____

_____

Understanding Cultural Differences

Sandy Cameron

Welcome to Camp Gateway

Welcome to another fun-filled summer at Camp Gateway. As you all know, Camp Gateway prides itself on attracting and bringing together campers and staff members from **diverse** cultural backgrounds. The unique opportunity our camp provides its campers and staff can be wonderfully rewarding, but it requires a spirit of trust, patience, and cooperation from every one of us. This pamphlet suggests a variety of ways in which we can be more respectful of our cultural differences and less likely to **offend** our fellow campers and staff members.

Cultural Perspective

Being sensitive to cultural differences often helps us avoid misunderstandings. For example, think about the many ways in which a simple smile might be interpreted, depending on one's cultural **perspective**. For someone born in the United States, a smile would probably be understood to show pleasure or happiness. In Japan, too, people smile when they are happy. But Japanese people also smile when they are confused or embarrassed. In some other Asian cultures, people smile to show disagreement, anger, and frustration. Some people from Asia will not smile for official photos, such as passport photos, because these are considered serious occasions. They want to appear to be taking the situation seriously.

---

diverse, different; completely unalike
offend, make someone angry or upset
perspective, point of view

Whether to establish eye contact varies around the world as well. People from many Asian and Latin American cultures avoid direct eye contact because looking directly at someone can seem disrespectful. An American person might think exactly the opposite—that it is disrespectful not to look someone in the eye. So think twice before you judge someone for meeting or not meeting your glance.

Overcoming Language Barriers

Language differences can make communication difficult, but you can do things to help get your point across. Talk slowly and clearly. It may sound obvious, but don't shout at people if they don't understand what you are saying. Say what you want to say in a different way or repeat your words more slowly. Use other methods of communication, such as making drawings or acting out your ideas.

When speaking, avoid using slang expressions. Slang is more difficult for someone who is not a native speaker of your language. Instead, use more formal language.

In many cultures, people have difficulty saying "no" to a request, and some people may say "yes" when their answer is really "no." To be respectful of this fact, phrase questions so that they do not require a yes-or-no answer. A question such as "Would you rather play tennis or shoot archery?" is easier for many people to answer truthfully than "Would you like to play tennis?"

_____

establish eye contact, look at someone directly in the eyes

Reading Strategy: Monitoring Comprehension

Underline a key term in the first paragraph on this page. Ask and answer a question about that term. **MARK THE TEXT**

_____

_____

_____

_____

Comprehension Check

Circle four things to do when a person does not understand what you are saying. Which of these would you use with someone who does not understand your language at all? **MARK THE TEXT**

_____

_____

Text Structure: Informational Pamphlet

An informational pamphlet often gives tips or advice and examples to make those tips clearer. Underline the tip in the last paragraph, and circle the example that makes it clearer. What tip does the next-to-last paragraph give? What example might you use to make it clearer? **MARK THE TEXT**

_____

_____

Comprehension Check

Underline the key advice about names in the first paragraph. Why do you think it is important to learn to pronounce a person's name correctly?

MARK THE TEXT

_____

_____

_____

_____

_____

Reading Strategy: Monitoring Comprehension

Underline a key term in the second paragraph. Ask and answer a question about that term.

MARK THE TEXT

_____

_____

_____

_____

_____

Text Structure: Informational Pamphlet

Underline the words in the last paragraph that sum up the main information the pamphlet provides. What viewpoint about Camp Gateway does the pamphlet express?

MARK THE TEXT

_____

_____

_____

_____

Names and Time

People in the United States generally call others by their first names very soon after meeting them, but this is not true in all cultures. It's important to know what a person from another country prefers to be called. You should let others know what name they should call you. If necessary, pronounce each other's names slowly or write them down for each other.

Cultural backgrounds often dictate what people expect with regard to time and punctuality. What you consider to be on time, late, and early might be different from your fellow campers' and staff members' ideas. Don't be afraid to ask someone to clarify exactly when he or she expects you to be somewhere.

Learning about other cultures and being respectful of differences can go a long way toward ensuring that every camper and staff member has a rewarding and memorable experience here at Camp Gateway.

_____

punctuality, being on time
clarify, explain or make clear
go a long way toward, do a lot to; help to

Choose one and complete:
1. Draw a picture illustrating behavior that the pamphlet describes or recommends.
2. Create a glossary of common English slang terms and their meanings. The glossary might help non-native speakers learn more slang or help English speakers avoid slang.
3. Do research on the Internet to find out more about different customs around the world. List the customs and the cultures that practice them.

Retell It!

Develop a story about a camper at Camp Gateway. Explain how the advice in the pamphlet helps him or her correct or avoid mistakes with people from different cultures that he or she meets at the camp.

_____

_____

_____

_____

_____

_____

_____

_____

_____

_____

Reader's Response

Do you think this pamphlet will be useful to campers at Camp Gateway? Why or why not?

_____

_____

_____

_____

Think About the Skill

How did monitoring comprehension—by asking and answering questions—help you better understand the information in this pamphlet?

_____

_____

_____

_____

GRAMMAR

Use with textbook page 36.

Subject-Verb Agreement in the Simple Present
When you use the simple present, the subject and verb must "agree." This means when you use *he, she,* or *it,* the verb must end in *-s.*

Subject	Verb
I	help
We	help
They	help
He	helps
She	helps
It	helps

Circle the simple present verb and underline the subject in each sentence below. Then write *S* for singular or *P* for plural subject on the line.

_____ **1.** The Chinese students talk about the Americans constantly.

_____ **2.** The professor talks about American History.

_____ **3.** The lectures teach students about Chinese culture and history.

_____ **4.** I think about the differences in China and America often.

_____ **5.** She socializes more with students from other countries.

_____ **6.** In many countries, students begin to study other languages at a very

young age.

_____ **7.** Americans speak about political ideas without worrying.

_____ **8.** The student stays in the dormitory of the Institute.

_____ **9.** We really enjoy talking to Chinese students about their government.

_____ **10.** The journalist discusses cultural values and politics.

GRAMMAR

Use after the lesson on question forms in the present and past.

Question Forms: Present/Past

Use a verb in the simple present to ask questions about what is happening now.

How <u>are</u> you?   <u>Do</u> you know him?   When <u>are</u> you going?

Use a verb in the simple past to ask questions about something that has already happened.

How <u>was</u> school yesterday?   <u>Did</u> you see him?   When <u>did</u> you go?

Underline the verb in each question. Decide if the question asks about something in the present or the past. Circle the word *present* or *past* in parentheses ( ).

Example: Who <u>do</u> you see in the classroom? (present / past)

1. How many people are at the Chinese American Institute? (present / past)

2. Where did you study last week? (present / past)

3. Are you happy with your classes? (present / past)

4. What was Lingdi's job in the government? (present / past)

5. When do the Americans at the Institute study? (present / past)

6. Did you understand the professor's lecture about China? (present / past)

7. Where do Chinese and American students and faculty live? (present / past)

8. Who were the students in your English language class? (present/past)

9. When did you first hear about this program? (present / past)

10. How do you feel about Chinese / American

    relations now? (present / past)

SKILLS FOR WRITING

Use with textbook page 37.

Writing Journal Entries to Develop Fluency
A journal is a collection of writings about your experiences, thoughts and feelings.
Read the journal entry below and answer the questions about it.

June 18

My cousin from Taiwan finally arrived today. She was supposed to be
here two weeks ago. She got sick and her trip was delayed. I was so
excited to see her. I hadn't seen her in twelve years. Back then, we were
both just little kids. Now we're both grown up.

Her name is Mei. At first, I didn't think that she understood what I
was saying. I got frustrated. I wanted to tell her so much, but she just
looked at me and said, "What?" It just took a little while for her to get
used to our English. By the afternoon, neither of us could stop talking.
She told me what things are like in Taipei and how they're the same and
different from here. She'll be here all summer. It'll be just like having the
sister I always wanted!

1. How does the date at the beginning of the journal entry help the reader?

_____

_____

2. What event does the entry describe? How does the writer feel about this event?

_____

_____

3. What feelings or emotions does the writer describe?

_____

_____

4. List three things you learn about the writer from this journal entry.

_____

_____

5. What do you find out about the visiting cousin?

_____

_____

PROOFREADING AND EDITING

Use with textbook page 38.

Read the story carefully. Find all the mistakes. Then rewrite the story below correctly on the lines.

my Funny Cousin

Have you met my cousin Mei? She is so much fun! When the radio alarm clock goes off and play a song, Mei doesn't try to go back to sleep. She jumps out of bed and starts singing and dancing. that sure wakes everyone up!

At breakfast, Mei always put a teaspoon of hot pepper on her scrambled eggs. Then she fans her mouth and drink about a gallon of water. i ask her why she puts so much pepper on if it's too hot. She says she like it

Mei does a funny thing when she gets dressed, too. she always wear two different-colored socks! My mom say that she must have another pair just like it

these are a few things Mei does in the morning, but Mei is funny all day long! She is my best friend!

_____

_____

_____

_____

_____

_____

_____

_____

_____

_____

SPELLING

Use after the spelling lesson.

Spelling Long and Short e, o, u
Here are spellings and example words for the long vowel sounds e, o, u.

long e	**e_e, ee, ea, e**	gene, beef, neat, we
long o	**o_e, oa, ow, o**	tone, boat, row, so
long u	**u_e, ew, ue, u**	tube, drew, blue, duty

Here are the spelling and example words for the short vowels e, o, u.

short e	**e** pet
short o	**o** pot
short u	**u** tub

Answer each riddle with a word from the box. Then circle the letters that spell the long or short vowel sound. (Hint: You will not use all the words.)

joke	hope	plead	sun	coat	retribution	continue	between	she
just	attend	knock	shun	phone	bud	boast	sheet	toll

Example: I have long o. I rhyme with cone.   _ph**o**ne_

1. I have long e spelled ee. I rhyme with screen. _____

2. I have long o spelled o_e. I rhyme with spoke. _____

3. I have long u spelled ue. I rhyme with blue. _____

4. I have long e spelled ea. I rhyme with bead. _____

5. I have long e spelled e. I rhyme with we. _____

6. I have long u spelled u. I rhyme with solution. _____

7. I have long o spelled oa. I rhyme with goat. _____

8. I have short e spelled e. I rhyme with mend. _____

9. I have short o spelled o. I rhyme with stock. _____

10. I have short u spelled u. I rhyme with mud. _____

UNIT 2 The Human Spirit

PART 1

Contents

VOCABULARY

Use with textbook page 49.

Use the context of each sentence to choose the word that best completes it. Choose from the words and phrases in the box. You will use each word or phrase once.

unity	took a stand	refused	losses	hardship

1. Abraham Lincoln _____ to let being poor stop him from getting an education.

2. Lincoln suffered a great deal of _____ during his life.

3. He _____ against slavery because he believed it was wrong.

4. Families of soldiers experienced many _____ during the Civil War.

5. After the Civil War, the divided country had to work towards _____ .

Read the clues. Use the words in the box to complete the crossword puzzle. (Hint: You will not use all of the words.)

hardship	political	refused	assassination	abolish
expansion	unity	abolitionists	slave	educated

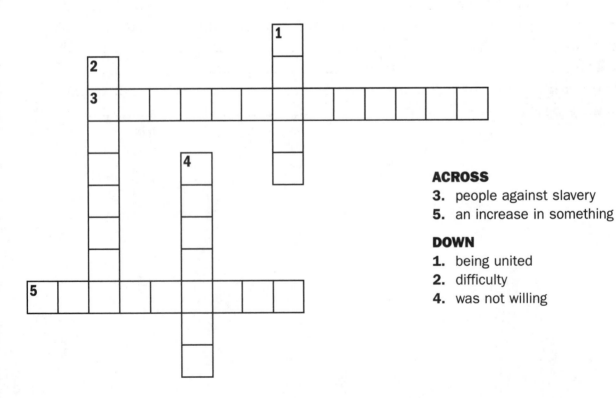

ACROSS
3. people against slavery
5. an increase in something

DOWN
1. being united
2. difficulty
4. was not willing

Unit 2 The Human Spirit Part 1

VOCABULARY BUILDING

Understanding Suffixes

A **suffix** is a word part added to the end of a base word. Adding a suffix changes the word's meaning.

The suffix **-ion** means "act of." If the base word ends in an e, drop the e before adding -ion.

Verb	+ Suffix	= Noun	Meaning
elect	-ion	election	the act of electing
emancipate	-ion	emancipation	the act of freeing someone

The suffix **-ship** means "state or quality of being."

Word	+ Suffix	= New Word	Meaning
hard	-ship	hardship	being in a state of difficulty
friend	-ship	friendship	state of being a friend

The suffix **-ness** means "state or quality of being." If the base word ends in y, change it to an i.

Word	+ Suffix	= New Word	Meaning
happy	-ness	happiness	state of being happy
good	-ness	goodness	quality of being good

Make new words by combining a suffix and a base word. Write a definition for each. Use a dictionary if necessary. Follow the example.

Word + Suffix	New Word	Definition
restrict + ion	*restriction*	*the act of restricting someone*

1. assassinate + ion _____ _____

2. citizen + ship _____ _____

3. educate + ion _____ _____

4. reconstruct + ion _____ _____

5. sad + ness _____ _____

READING STRATEGY

Use with textbook page 49.

Taking Notes

Taking notes helps you remember important facts more easily. When you take notes, don't write complete sentences. Use abbreviations whenever you can. As you take notes, keep your purpose for reading in mind.

Read the first three paragraphs of *Abraham Lincoln* on pages 50–51 in your textbook. As you read, use the questions below to help you take notes about the most important facts. Write your notes in the space provided.

	Notes
1. What is your purpose for reading about Abraham Lincoln?	
2. When and where was Lincoln born?	
3. What kind of education did Lincoln's parents have?	
4. What important job did Lincoln finally get?	
5. Why was reading so important to Lincoln's life?	

Use with textbook pages 58–60.

Summary: "Nancy Hanks" and "Lincoln"

Nancy Hanks was Abraham Lincoln's mother. She died when Lincoln was only nine years old. The poem "Nancy Hanks" is an imaginary conversation that she might have had, asking someone what happened to her son. The poem "Lincoln" compares Abraham Lincoln to a giant pine tree protecting the United States.

Visual Summary

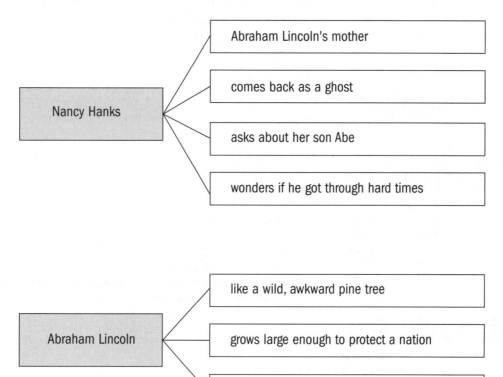

Nancy Hanks
- Abraham Lincoln's mother
- comes back as a ghost
- asks about her son Abe
- wonders if he got through hard times

Abraham Lincoln
- like a wild, awkward pine tree
- grows large enough to protect a nation
- struck down by a mad stray bolt of lightning

Nancy Hanks

Rosemary Carr and Stephen Vincent Benét

Use What You Know

Name a person who is important in a young child's life. Tell why.

_____

_____

_____

_____

_____

Text Structure: Poem

Poems express emotions, experiences, and ideas. They are presented in lines that are often grouped into stanzas. Circle the first stanza of this poem. How many lines are there in each stanza?

MARK THE TEXT

_____

Literary Element: Rhyme

Words that rhyme have the same final sounds. For example, *ghost* and *most* rhyme. Poets often use rhymes at the ends of lines. Circle three other pairs of rhymes at the ends of lines in this poem, and connect your circles to show each pair. What do the rhyming words in this poem help you focus on?

MARK THE TEXT

_____

_____

_____

_____

_____

If Nancy Hanks
Came back as a **ghost**,
Seeking news
Of what she loved most,
She'd ask first
"Where's my son?
What's happened to Abe?
What's he done?

"Poor little Abe
Left all alone
Except for Tom
Who's a **rolling stone**:
He was only nine
The year I died,
I remember still
How hard he cried.

_____

ghost, the spirit of a dead person
rolling stone, someone who doesn't stay in one place for very long; someone who wanders around

"Scraping along
In a little shack,
With hardly a shirt
To cover his back,
And a prairie wind
To blow him down,
Or pinching times
If he went to town.

"You wouldn't know
About my son?
Did he grow tall?
Did he have fun?
Did he learn to read?
Did he get to town?
Do you know his name?
Did he get on?"

_____

scraping along, trying to survive without much money
shack, a very small poorly built house, usually one room
prairie, a big field covered with wild grass and flowers
pinching times, a time when you have very little money or food
get on, do well

Reading Strategy: Visualizing

Visualizing means picturing something you read or hear about. Poets use words that help you visualize what they write. Circle two details in the next-to-last stanza that help you visualize young Abraham Lincoln. From these details, what can you conclude about his early life?

_____

_____

_____

Comprehension Check

Underline the questions Nancy Hanks asks about her son in the last stanza. How do you think she would feel if she knew the answers?

_____

_____

_____

Text Structure: Poem

The rhymes in some poems form a pattern followed in every stanza. Determine the pattern of rhymes in "Nancy Hanks." In each stanza, which lines end in words that rhyme with each other?

_____

_____

_____

_____

Lincoln
John Gould Fletcher

Like a **gaunt**, **scraggly** pine
Which lifts its head above the **mournful**
    sandhills;
And patiently, through dull years of
    bitter silence,
Untended and uncared for, starts to grow.

Ungainly, **laboring**, huge,
The wind of the north has twisted and
    gnarled its branches;
Yet in the heat of mid-summer days,
    when thunder clouds ring the horizon,
A nation of men shall rest beneath its shade.

And it shall protect them all,
Hold everyone safe there, watching **aloof**
    in silence.
Until at last, one **mad stray bolt** from the
    zenith
Shall strike it in an instant down to earth.

---

gaunt, very thin and bony
scraggly, rough; irregular
mournful, very sad
ungainly, awkward; clumsy
laboring, working very hard
aloof, away from or distant from
mad stray bolt, an unexpected flash of lightning
zenith, the sky; the highest point

Literary Element: Simile

A simile uses *like* or *as* to compare two unlike things. In "Lincoln," a simile about Lincoln introduced early in the poem is then extended, with more details added. Underline the basic simile in the line where it is introduced. Over how many lines is that simile extended?

 MARK THE TEXT

_____

Reading Strategy: Visualizing

Circle five details that help you visualize the tree that Lincoln is compared with. What do the details in the first stanza tell you about Lincoln's early life?

 MARK THE TEXT

_____

_____

What do the details in the second stanza tell you about Lincoln's relationship with the nation?

_____

_____

Comprehension Check

Underline the force that destroys the tree. What event does this represent in Lincoln's life?

MARK THE TEXT

_____

_____

What do the words *mad* and *stray* emphasize about it?

_____

_____

Choose one and complete:
1. Write a letter to Nancy Hanks answering her questions about her son. Use biographical references or the Internet for information about Lincoln.
2. Paint or draw the tree compared to Lincoln in the second poem.
3. Imagine you are reciting one of these two poems in a group presentation. Describe the background music you might use to help capture the mood.

Retell It!

Retell one of the poems in paragraph form, using your own words.

_____

_____

_____

_____

_____

_____

_____

Reader's Response

Did the poems change your views about Abraham Lincoln or make you more interested in his life? If so, how? If not, why not?

_____

_____

_____

_____

_____

_____

Think About the Skill

How did visualizing help you better appreciate the poems?

_____

_____

_____

_____

_____

GRAMMAR

Use with textbook page 62.

Using Real Conditionals: Sentences with *if* Clauses
Real conditional sentences include a **main clause** and an ***if* clause.**

- The *if* clause states a condition that may or may not happen.
- The main clause states the result (or possible result) of that condition.
- An *if* clause can go before or after the main clause. Use a comma when the if clause comes before the main clause.

	Verb in *if* Clause	Verb in Main Clause	Example
Events that *usually* happen	Use a simple present verb.	Use a simple present verb.	If there **is** a program on TV about the Civil War, I **watch** it.
Events that *might* happen in the future	Use a simple present verb.	Use a simple future verb.	If the program about the Civil War **is** on TV tomorrow night, I **will watch** it.

Complete each sentence by using the correct form of the verb in parentheses ( ).Write the correct form of the verb in the space provided.

1. If I don't understand my history homework, I (ask) _____ my brother for help.

2. If my brother is too busy, I (call) _____ my uncle.

3. I (study) _____ tomorrow night if there is a test on Friday.

4. I often (use) _____ the Internet if I need information.

5. I (pass) _____ the history exam on Friday if I study hard.

Unit 2   The Human Spirit   Part 1

GRAMMAR

Use after the lesson on parts of speech.

Identifying Parts of Speech

There are eight main **parts of speech** in the English language. Match each definition with the examples that go with it. Write the appropriate letter in the space provided.

_____ 1. A **noun** names a person, place, or thing.　　**a.** it, he, you

_____ 2. A **verb** shows action or a state of being.　　**b.** Lincoln, Kentucky, cabin

_____ 3. A **pronoun** takes the place of a noun.　　**c.** lifted, grew, protect, is

_____ 4. An **adjective** describes a noun or pronoun.　　**d.** great, huge, famous

_____ 5. An **adverb** describes a verb, adjective, or adverb.　　**e.** wow, oh, gee

_____ 6. A **conjunction** links words or parts of a sentence.　　**f.** patiently, instantly, always

_____ 7. A **preposition** tells where, in what direction, or when.　　**g.** and, but, or

_____ 8. An **interjection** expresses a strong feeling.　　**h.** in, to, after

Read the sentences. Circle the verbs. Draw one line under the nouns. Draw two lines under the adjectives. Draw three lines under the pronoun. Put a box around the preposition.

9. Lincoln lived in a small, dark cabin.

10. He never received a formal education.

SKILLS FOR WRITING

Use with textbook page 63.

Persuasive Writing

When you **write to persuade**, think about these questions:
- Who are you trying to persuade?
- What is your opinion?
- What arguments are important to your readers?

Read the persuasive paragraph below. Answer the questions in the space provided.

    I believe that people like you can improve your lives through reading. If you read a lot, you also learn a lot. Abraham Lincoln is a perfect example of this. He didn't have much schooling, but he loved to read. He educated himself by reading books about many different topics. He taught himself to be a lawyer. Finally, he was elected President of the United States. I think you should all be like Abe Lincoln. You can find success through reading.

1. What is the topic of this paragraph? _____

_____

_____

2. Who is the writer trying to persuade? _____

_____

_____

3. What is the writer's opinion? _____

_____

_____

4. What argument does the writer use? _____

_____

_____

5. Do you think the writer succeeds in persuading the reader? Why or why not?

_____

_____

PROOFREADING AND EDITING

Use with textbook page 64.

Read the persuasive essay carefully. Find the mistakes. Rewrite the essay correctly on the lines below. Make sure you correct all the mistakes!

Should students Study History?

today, many students don't want to study events that happened a long time ago. They thnk history is boring They believe that knowing the name of past presidents isn't important. if history classes are abolished today we will be sorry tomorrow. It is important to study the past. History classes should connect more to students' lives. we need to show how exciting the pst really was. If history classes don't improve soon, students continue to moan about studying "former presdents." But if students learn about history today, they improve the future tomorrow.

_____

_____

_____

_____

_____

_____

_____

_____

_____

_____

_____

_____

_____

_____

SPELLING

Use after the spelling lesson.

Spelling with Double *l* and *r*

Double *l* can occur in the middle or at the end of a word. Words rarely begin with double *l*.

dull   killed   pull   allow

Double *r* can occur in the middle or at the end of a word. Words cannot begin with a double *r*.

terrible   borrow   territory   purr

Complete the chart. Write the words from the box below under the correct heading. Then circle the double *l* or double *r* in each word.

territories	still	purr	marrying	fill	William	worry	burr
borrow	chill	sorry	illegal	spill	shallow	allow	follow
Illinois	err	all	terrible				

Double *l* in the middle	Double *l* at the end	Double *r* in the middle	Double *r* at the end
1. Follow	7. still	12. territories	18. burr
2. Allow	8. chill	13. borrow	19. purr
3. William	9. all	14. sorry	20. err
4. Shallow	10. fill	15. terrible	
5. illegal	11. spill	16. Marrying	
6. Illinois		17. worry	

UNIT 2 The Human Spirit

PART 2

Contents

VOCABULARY

Use with textbook page 67.

Use the context of each sentence to choose the word that best completes it. Choose from the words and phrases in the box. You will use each word or phrase once.

| encouragement | defended | approve of | criticizing | remarkable |

1. Sor Juana Inés de la Cruz _____ the rights of woman to

   study and learn.

2. Her grandfather gave her a lot of _____ and support

   when she was young.

3. The forty scholars thought it was _____ that such a

   young woman knew so much.

4. Some men in the church did not _____ Sor Juana

   because she wrote about things other than religion.

5. Sor Juana made the archbishop angry when she wrote a letter

   _____ a priest's sermon.

Read the clues. Use the words in the box to complete the crossword puzzle. (Hint: You will not use all the words.)

| remarkable | dowry | recreation | stump | gossip | epidemic | advice | defended |

ACROSS
1. suggestion about what should be done
4. extraordinary
5. an outbreak of disease that spreads quickly

DOWN
2. the money or property a bride brings to her husband at marriage
3. protected from harm

VOCABULARY BUILDING

Understanding Homophones

Homophones are words that sound the same but are spelled differently and have different meanings.

poor/pour	nun /none
She is **poor**, not rich. Please **pour** me some water.	Juana became a **nun**. I wanted to give you a book about Sor Juana, but **none** were left.
two/to/too	write/right
She lived in **two** different cities. I lived in Mexico City, **too**. I moved **to** the U.S. when I was young.	Juana learned to read and **write**. What is the **right** answer?
knew/new	would/wood
I **knew** all the answers in class today. He finally saved enough to buy a **new** car.	She **would** see a movie if her friend came along. He went outside to chop **wood** for the fire.

Circle the homophone in parentheses ( ) that correctly completes each sentence.

1. Juana grew up with her mother and (two/to/too) sisters.

2. She was (poor/pour) and had few things when she was a little girl.

3. Juana entered the San Jerónimo convent and became a (none/nun).

4. Later in life she began to (right/write) poetry.

5. Words began to (poor/pour) from her pen.

6. Some people did not think it was (right/write) for a woman to be so educated.

7. Juana (knew/new) what she had to do.

8. She (wood/would) always follow her beliefs.

9. (To/Too/Two) many people, she was a hero.

10. Now people are writing about her, (to/too/two) .

READING STRATEGY

Use with textbook page 67.

Making Inferences

Good readers **make inferences** as they read. They make logical guesses about what is happening. To make inferences, readers use what the author says and their own experience.

Read the first two paragraphs of *Sor Juana Inés de la Cruz* on pages 68–69 in your textbook. The author never tells the reader how Juana feels about her grandfather. Readers have to infer this detail using the text and their own experiences. Here is an inference that one reader made about Juana.

Details from Text		Personal Knowledge or Experience		Inferences
Juana lived with her grandfather. He was a gentle man who liked books. Juana liked books too.	+	I wonder how Juana feels about her grandfather. I know that I love my grandparents and that they influence me in the things I do.	=	Juana must love her grandfather a lot because they both liked books and earning.

Read the rest of page 69 in your textbook. Answer the questions.

1. What inferences can you make about the fact that Juana was poor, but became the

   greatest poet in Mexico? _____

   _____

2. What inferences can you make about the kind of person Juana's mother was?

   _____

   _____

3. What inferences can you make about how Juana felt about her grandfather's death?

   _____

   _____

4. What inferences can you make about how Juana probably felt about the vicereine?

   _____

   _____

5. What inferences can you make about how Juana felt about life at the viceregal

   court? _____

   _____

Use with textbook pages 76–78.

Summary: "The Peace Corps"

This passage tells about the Peace Corps, an American organization that helps people in other countries. Peace Corps volunteers build houses and schools. They teach farmers about ways to grow food. They help people get clean water and learn ways to fight diseases. The volunteers learn from the people and places they visit, and they share their knowledge and experiences with others when they return to the United States.

Visual Summary

Who?	President John F. Kennedy
What?	established Peace Corps
When?	1961
Why?	to promote world peace and friendship
How?	by sending volunteers to help communities improve social, educational, and economic conditions
Where?	developing countries around the world

Use What You Know

List two things you know about organizations that help people around the world.

1. _____

2. _____

Text Structure: Social Studies Article

Social studies articles often give information about historical events and their relationships. Underline the first year mentioned in this article and the event that took place then. How is this event related to the Peace Corps?

MARK THE TEXT

_____

_____

_____

_____

_____

_____

Reading Strategy: Taking Notes

When you take notes, you write down important information. You can use incomplete sentences, abbreviations, and symbols as long as you will understand them later. Circle ideas and details in the first three sentences that you would include in your notes. What two terms might you abbreviate, and how?

MARK THE TEXT

1. _____

2. _____

The Peace Corps

Shortly after John F. Kennedy became president in 1961, he established the Peace Corps. The Peace Corps is an **agency** that **promotes** world peace and friendship. Volunteers from the United States work in communities in **developing** countries. They help these communities improve social, educational, and economic conditions. Peace Corps volunteers help to build schools; they teach; they help farmers; they help to bring clean water to communities; they work to stop the spread of AIDS and other diseases. These are just a few examples of the ways volunteers try to help.

_____

agency, an organization, especially within a government, that does a specific job
promotes, helps something develop and be successful
developing, growing or changing into a country with a lot of industry

Choose one and complete:
1. Draw a picture of a Peace Corps volunteer helping in a community overseas.
2. Draw a map of the world showing nations where America sends Peace Corps volunteers. Check your facts on the Internet.
3. Do research to find out more about being a volunteer in the Peace Corps. Then, pretend to be someone just back from serving in the Peace Corps. Describe what your time in the Peace Corps was like.

More than 165,000 Americans have joined the Peace Corps, and they have worked in more than 100 countries. Volunteers must be at least eighteen years old. But adults of all ages join, including senior citizens . Volunteers receive language and cross-cultural training when they go to the countries where they will work. They are expected to speak the local language, to respect the customs of the people they work with, and to adapt to the living conditions of the communities in which they work.

One of the goals of the Peace Corps is to help give the people in developing countries the education and training needed to take care of their own futures. The Peace Corps tries to focus on the most important needs of the countries where the organization is active. For example, in countries where most people need to get their food directly from their land, the focus is on farming and agriculture, rather than business or education.

Since 1995, the Peace Corps has also worked with the International Rescue Committee (IRC). Together, the IRC and the Peace Corps help refugees by providing useful training such as farming methods that don't harm the environment. The countries where the two organizations have worked together include Tanzania, Rwanda, and Burundi in Africa.

---

senior citizens, people over sixty-five years old
adapt, change your behavior because of a new situation you are in
focus, concentrate; place importance
refugees, people who have to leave their own countries, especially because of a war
harm, hurt

Reading Strategy: Taking Notes

Organizing your notes by topic will make them easier to use later. Underline two details in the first two sentences that you would include in notes about the topic "volunteers." What words in the second sentence might you write in a shorter way? How would you write them?

_____

_____

_____

_____

Comprehension Check

Circle a goal of the Peace Corps mentioned in the second paragraph. Where does the Peace Corps focus on farming and agriculture?

_____

_____

_____

**Text Structure:
Social Studies Article**

Social studies includes not only history but geography, the study of places around the world. Underline three countries where the Peace Corps and the IRC have worked together. On what continent are these countries located?

_____

Comprehension Check

Underline three criticisms of the Peace Corps in the first paragraph. Which of these criticisms is discussed more in the next paragraph?

MARK THE TEXT

_____

_____

Reading Strategy: Taking Notes

Circle two things that the second paragraph says Peace Corps workers do. If you were including these details in your notes, with what topic or heading would you list them?

MARK THE TEXT

_____

_____

Comprehension Check

Underline the opinion about our planet expressed in the third paragraph. How does the Peace Corps help strengthen the connections mentioned in the paragraph?

MARK THE TEXT

_____

_____

_____

_____

_____

_____

Some people criticize the Peace Corps because they think volunteers don't receive enough training. They think Peace Corps volunteers do not stay long enough in the countries they visit to really understand local problems. Some people also believe that Americans should spend their time and energy working on problems here in our own country.

Some volunteers actually do try to help make life better for others here in the United States. They believe their experience in other countries helps them to do this. Volunteers learn many things from the people in their host countries. Often, when they return to the United States, they continue to promote peace and understanding. There is a program called The Peace Corps Fellows/USA that helps volunteers get **scholarships** for master's degree programs when they return. In exchange, the returned volunteers teach or work in other areas such as public health. The Peace Corps also helps Americans understand different cultures and countries. For example, some returned volunteers visit schools and talk to students about their experiences. Students have the opportunity to ask volunteers questions about places they are studying.

Now, more than ever, we realize how **interconnected** we all are, here on our planet. Peace Corps volunteers and the people they work and live with help to strengthen these connections.

The IRC helps people who are leaving a country because they are being harmed because of their race, culture, or religion. They also help people whose countries have been struck by war or violence. They provide medical services and a safe place for people to live.

_____

scholarships, money given to students to help pay for their education
interconnected, linked together

Retell It!

Imagine that you are a Peace Corps worker keeping a diary. List some of the experiences, thoughts, and feelings that you might record in your diary.

_____

_____

_____

_____

_____

_____

_____

Reader's Response

Based on what you've read, what do you think of the Peace Corps? Why?

_____

_____

_____

_____

_____

_____

Think About the Skill

How did taking notes help improve your understanding of this informational text?

_____

_____

_____

_____

_____

GRAMMAR

Use with textbook page 80.

Using Modals of Advice

Use the **modals of advice** *should, shouldn't, had better,* and *had better not* to give advice in English. Modals go before the base form of a verb.

Kind of Advice	Modal to Use
To advise someone to do something	More people **should** join the Peace Corps.
To advise someone not to do something	Interested people **shouldn't** be afraid to ask questions.
A stronger way to advise someone to do something	The students **had better** study.
A stronger way to advise someone not to do something	They **had better not** be late for the meeting.
Two ways to make advice more polite	**I think** you should go. **Maybe** you should go.

Complete each sentence with the modal described in parentheses ( ). Use the chart to help you.

1. You _____ consider volunteering. (Give advice.)

2. You _____ be worried about trying something new. (Give advice not

   to do something.)

3. They _____ pack their suitcases carefully. (Give stronger advice.)

4. Peace Corps volunteers _____ be late for their flights. (Give

   stronger advice not to do something.)

5. _____ you should try to serve your community. (Make the advice

   more polite.)

Unit 2   The Human Spirit   Part 1

Name _____ Date _____

Use after the lesson on adjective clauses.

Adjective Clauses

A clause is a group of words that has a subject and a verb but may not express a complete thought. An **adjective clause** adds detail to a sentence by giving more information about a noun. Adjective clauses usually begin with one of the relative pronouns: *who, whom, whose, which,* or *that.*

> I know someone **who** *joined the Peace Corps.*
> The organization, **which** *was established in* 1961, helps people in developing countries.
> They teach farming methods **that** *don't harm the environment.*

Underline the adjective clause in each sentence.
On the line, write the noun that the clause describes.

Example: We met a Peace Corps volunteer who is living in Ecuador. ___*volunteer*___

1. The speaker who came to our school works for the Peace Corps.

   _____

2. She discussed projects that teach safe farming. _____

3. The students to whom she spoke were very interested. _____

4. Her speech, which was taped, will be broadcast next week. _____

5. I liked the reporter, whose questions were very interesting. _____

6. President Kennedy founded the Peace Corps, which still exists. _____

7. One woman who joined the Peace Corps was seventy. _____

8. The article that I read about Mali was fascinating. _____

9. The children, whose food was grown by volunteers, were healthy. _____

10. My neighbor, who is from Africa, worked with the Peace Corps. _____

SKILLS FOR WRITING

Use with textbook page 81.

Giving Advice in an Informal E-mail Message

You can use an e-mail message to give advice. The language in an e-mail is often informal. It sounds very casual, as if you are speaking to a friend.

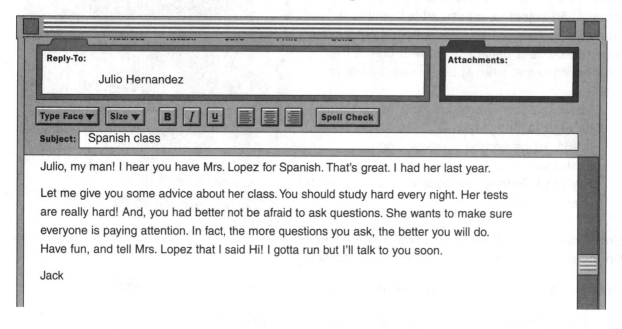

Answer the questions about the e-mail message.

1. Where does the writer tell what the e-mail is about? _____

2. How does the writer begin the e-mail message? Is this formal or informal language?

_____

_____

3. What does the writer advise his friend to do? _____

_____

4. What does the writer advise his friend not to do? _____

_____

5. What is another example of informal language used in the e-mail message?

_____

_____

PROOFREADING AND EDITING

Use with textbook page 82.

Read the e-mail message below carefully. Find the mistakes. Rewrite the e-mail message correctly on the lines below.

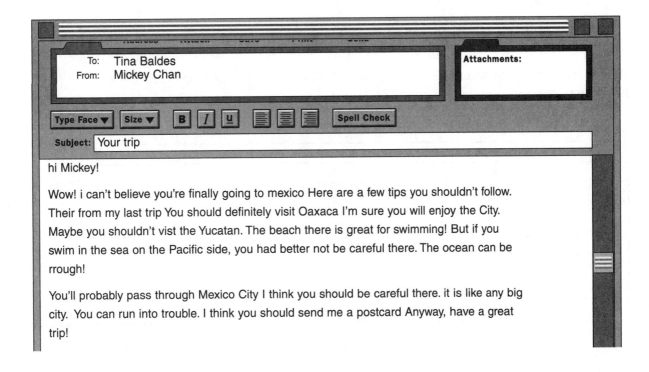

To: Tina Baldes
From: Mickey Chan

Attachments:

Type Face ▼   Size ▼   B   I   U   Spell Check

Subject: Your trip

hi Mickey!

Wow! i can't believe you're finally going to mexico Here are a few tips you shouldn't follow. Their from my last trip You should definitely visit Oaxaca I'm sure you will enjoy the City. Maybe you shouldn't vist the Yucatan. The beach there is great for swimming! But if you swim in the sea on the Pacific side, you had better not be careful there. The ocean can be rrough!

You'll probably pass through Mexico City I think you should be careful there. it is like any big city. You can run into trouble. I think you should send me a postcard Anyway, have a great trip!

To: _____

Subject: _____

_____

_____

_____

_____

_____

_____

_____

_____

SPELLING

Use after the spelling lesson.

Spelling Words With Initial *W* and *J*

In English, the letter *j* at the beginning of a word is pronounced like the sound at the beginning of the word *jump*: *jet, jam, justice*.

The letter *w* at the beginning of a word is pronounced like the sound at the beginning of the word *wish*: *will, want, world*.

Read the words in the box. Write them in the chart beneath the word with the same beginning sound.

| were   juice   would   John   jury   worked   jungle   wall   water   just |

Just	Well
1. _____	6. _____
2. _____	7. _____
3. _____	8. _____
4. _____	9. _____
5. _____	10. _____

Unit 2   The Human Spirit   Part 1

UNIT **3** Voices of Freedom

PART 1

Contents

VOCABULARY

Use with textbook page 93.

Complete the sentences by circling the words in parentheses that make the most sense.

1. His good (character / rights) kept him from doing wrong.

2. Because of (confusion / segregation), the two groups could not spend time together.

3. The angry American colonists started a (revolt / rumor) against the British government.

4. This dictator is known for the terrible (oppression / fairness) and cruel treatment of his subjects.

5. Employers should avoid (poverty / discrimination) and treat all employees fairly.

Read the clues. Use the words in the box to complete the crossword puzzle. (Hint: You will not use all of the words.)

| refuse | oppression | employment | speech | revolt |
| poverty | segregation | educational | justice | leader |

ACROSS
1. cruel and unjust treatment
3. keeping groups of people apart
5. fair treatment

DOWN
2. the state of being poor
4. to fight against those with power

VOCABULARY BUILDING

Understanding *Have* + Noun

The word *have* (and its forms *has* and *had*) can be used as a helper for a verb. For example, *I have seen Martin Luther King.* It can also be the main verb. When it is used as the main verb, it tells something about a noun, and it can have several different meanings.

a. To possess or own something	I **have** a new **book** by my favorite author. Our school **has** a brand new **gym**.
b. To contain something	The cafeteria burritos **have beans** in them. The paint **has** no **lead** in it.
c. To arrange something	**Have** the new **student** sit in the chair by the window. Let's **have** the **party** on Thursday after school.
d. To eat something	I **had dinner** already. Did you **have cake**?
e. To experience something	I **had** a **dream** that I spoke Russian perfectly. The students **had** a good **time** at the school play.

Compare each sentence with the sentences in the chart above. Decide what the verb *have, has,* or *had* tells about the noun in **boldfaced** type. Write the letter of the correct description in the space provided.

_____ **1.** The students *have* new **lockers**.

_____ **2.** The school *has* twenty **classrooms** in it.

_____ **3.** At ten o'clock, *have* **everyone** move to the buses.

_____ **4.** We *had* a great **time** at the class picnic.

_____ **5.** I *had* a submarine **sandwich** for lunch.

_____ **6.** Maria Elena *has* new tennis **shoes**.

_____ **7.** Armando *had* **fun** at the picnic.

_____ **8.** Mother *has* a **headache** from the hot sun.

_____ **9.** We can *have* the next **picnic** at the park again.

_____ **10.** I *had* only ten **minutes** to get home in time.

READING STRATEGY

Use with textbook page 93.

Summarizing

When you **summarize** a text, you briefly retell the main ideas in your own words. Use the following suggestions to summarize.

- As you read, ask questions and look for the author's main points.
- Look for the most important details that support the main ideas.
- Retell the main ideas and those details.

Read the two paragraphs in the "Make Connections" section on page 92. Then answer the questions to help you summarize the paragraphs.

1st Paragraph:

1. Main idea: What problems were African Americans facing in the 1950s and 1960s?

_____

2. Detail: Who was one of their leaders?

_____

2nd Paragraph:

3. Main idea: What was the Civil Rights movement?

_____

_____

4. Detail: Why was Dr. Martin Luther King Jr. important to the movement?

_____

_____

Both Paragraphs:

5. Now use your answers to summarize the two paragraphs in your own words.

_____

_____

_____

_____

_____

_____

Use with textbook pages 102–104.

Summary: "Lady Freedom Among Us"

Dove's poem describes *Freedom*, the statue that sits atop the dome of the Capitol in Washington, D.C. It was taken down for cleaning in 1993, giving the poet a chance to see it up close. The poem describes the statue's appearance, explores what it stands for, and stresses the importance of freedom to every one of us.

Visual Summary

Who she is	The statue *Freedom*
Where she is	In Washington, D.C. Removed for cleaning from dome of Capitol
What she is like	A homeless person
What we should not do	Ignore her Forget her
What we should do	Recognize that she is one of us Respect what she represents

Copyright © 2004 by Pearson Education, Inc.

Use What You Know

Read the title of the poem. What does freedom mean to you? What might "Lady Freedom Among Us" mean? Write what you think the poem will be about.

_____

_____

_____

_____

Text Structure: Poem

Some poems have stanzas with a fixed number of lines and a pattern of rhymes at the ends of lines. Does this one? Explain.

_____

_____

_____

Explain what is unusual about the capitalization and punctuation in the poem.

_____

_____

_____

Reading Strategy: Compare and Contrast

Underline three things the speaker tells passers-by not to say to the statue *Freedom*. Explain how these words help compare the statue to a homeless person.

MARK THE TEXT

_____

_____

_____

Lady Freedom Among Us
Rita Dove

don't lower your eyes
or stare straight ahead to where
you think you ought to be going

don't mutter *oh no*
not another one
get a job fly a kite
go bury a bone

_____

mutter, speak or say words unclearly; mumble

Choose one and complete:
1. Draw a picture of the *Freedom* statue based on the details in the poem.
2. Do research in library sources or on the Internet to find out more about the history of the statue. Take notes on the information you find.
3. Imagine you were in charge of a special event in which the statue was put back on the Capitol building after being cleaned. Describe the people who might speak or perform, the music that might play, the decorations you might use, or other arrangements you might make.

with her old-fashioned sandals
with her leaden skirts
with her stained cheeks and whiskers
    and heaped up trinkets
she has risen among us in blunt reproach

she has fitted her hair under a hand-me-down cap
and spruced it up with feathers and stars
slung over one shoulder she bears
the rainbowed layers of charity and murmurs
all of you even the least of you

don't cross to the other side of the square
don't think *another item to fit on a tourist's agenda*
consider her drenched gaze her shining brow
she who has brought mercy back into the streets
and will not retire politely to the potter's field

---

leaden, made of lead; heavy
blunt reproach, clear blame or disapproval
murmurs, whispers
square, an open place in a town with buildings all around it
potter's field, a burial place for very poor, unknown people

Literary Element: Metaphor

A metaphor compares two unlike things without using *like* or *as* to make the comparison. To what does this poem compare the statue *Freedom*?

_____

Circle three details that describe the statue's clothing or appearance. How do these details extend the comparison?

MARK THE TEXT

_____

_____

Comprehension Check

Underline what the speaker says the statue has brought back into the streets. Who do you think murmurs *"all of you even the least of you,"* the statue or the passers-by? Why?

MARK THE TEXT

_____

_____

_____

Reading Strategy: Compare and Contrast

Underline the place where the statue will not retire politely. What contrast does this make between the statue and a homeless person?

MARK THE TEXT

_____

_____

Comprehension Check

Underline the kind of skin the statue has gotten in "this town." What does getting this kind of skin mean?

_____

_____

What "town" does the speaker mean, and what do you think the speaker is saying about this town?

_____

_____

_____

_____

Reading Strategy: Compare and Contrast

Circle the words that tell why we can never forget her and what our only choice is. How does this contrast to what usually happens to a homeless person?

_____

_____

Comprehension Check

Underline what the speaker calls the statue in the last two lines. What do you think she might mean?

_____

_____

_____

having assumed the thick skin of this town
its gritted exhaust its sunscorched and **blear**
she rests in her weathered **plumage**
bigboned **resolute**

don't think you can ever forget her
don't even try
she's not going to **budge**

no choice but to grant her space
crown her with sky
for she is one of the many
and she is each of us

_____

blear, dim; sore
plumage, the feathers of a bird
resolute, determined; firm
budge, move; go away

Retell It!

Write a short newspaper article about the statue *Freedom* and what happened to it in 1993. In your article, describe the statue, using details from the poem. Then tell about the poem and the poet's viewpoint of the statue.

_____

_____

_____

_____

_____

_____

_____

Reader's Response

What new ideas did this poem give you about freedom, the United States, or homeless people?

_____

_____

_____

_____

_____

Think About the Skill

How did comparing and contrasting help you better understand the poem?

_____

_____

_____

_____

GRAMMAR

Use with textbook page 106.

The Present Perfect

The **simple past tense** tells about an action that happened at a specific time in the past.

> I **wrote** a letter to Dr. King when I was twelve years old.

The **present perfect tense** describes actions that happened sometime in the past. Form the present perfect with *have* or *has* and the past participle.

> I **have written** many fan letters to famous people in the last two years.

For each pair of sentences choose the verb in parentheses that completes each sentence.

1. She (bought / has bought) a book by Rita Dove yesterday.

2. In the past, she (bought / has bought) many other books by this poet.

3. We (attended / have attended) poetry readings since we were in grade school.

4. Last week, we (attended / have attended) a poetry reading by a famous African American poet.

5. Rita Dove (enjoyed / has enjoyed) her one year as Poet Laureate of the United States.

6. Over the years, she (enjoyed / has enjoyed) her many travels across the country, too.

7. When he was a student, Julio (wrote / has written) five wonderful poems about Mexico.

8. He (wrote / has written) many short stories about his experiences as a cowboy, too.

9. I (was / have been) a big admirer of Rita Dove's poetry for many years.

10. In 2003, I (was / have been) the main organizer of a writing festival.

GRAMMAR

Use after the lesson on past participles.

Past Participles

A **past participle** is a verb form. It is often used with a helping verb, such as *have, has,* or *had*. When a verb is regular, the past participle is the same as the simple past form.

Simple Past	**Past Participle**
The poems *inspired* me.	The poems have ***inspired*** me.
He *memorized* all of it.	He has ***memorized*** all of it.
The magazine *published* it.	The magazine has ***published*** it.

When a verb is irregular, the past participle is different from the simple past form.

Simple Past	**Past Participle**
He *spoke*.	He has ***spoken***.
They *wrote* together.	They have ***written*** it together.

Look at the past participle in each sentence. Circle *correct* if it is the correct form. Circle *incorrect* if it is the incorrect form.

1. Many poets have respond to Dr. King's speech.   correct   incorrect

2. My mother has marched with Dr. King.   correct   incorrect

3. We have refused to accept unfair laws.   correct   incorrect

4. Everyone has listened carefully to his words.   correct   incorrect

5. The crowd has wait for Dr. King's speech.   correct   incorrect

Complete each sentence with the past participle form of the verb in parentheses ( ). Use the examples at the top of the page if you do not know the past participle form.

6. Dr. King had _____ at many other rallies. (speak)

7. His words have _____ many listeners and readers. (inspire)

8. I have _____ his remarkable speech. (memorize)

9. Our class has _____ a memorial poem. (write)

10. We have _____ our poem in the local newspaper. (publish)

SKILLS FOR WRITING

Use with textbook page 107.

Writing Essays

An **essay** is a short nonfiction work about a topic. It usually begins with a statement that tells what the essay is about. The rest of the information in the essay presents details that support the main idea.

Reread the essay on page 107 in your textbook. Then answer the questions.

1. Look at the first sentence of this essay. It tells the main idea. What is the main idea of the essay?

   _____

   _____

2. Look for details in the first paragraph. How many computers, cars, and televisions did families like Peggy's have in the 1950s?

   _____

   _____

   _____

3. Look at the first sentence of the second paragraph. It tells what that paragraph is about. What is the main idea of the second paragraph?

   _____

   _____

   _____

4. Look for details in the second paragraph. In what ways does Peggy use her PC?

   _____

   _____

   _____

5. Look at the third paragraph. It gives a conclusion to the essay. What are Peggy's final thoughts about technology? Is her life better or worse?

   _____

   _____

   _____

PROOFREADING AND EDITING

Use with textbook page 108.

Read the essay carefully. Find the mistakes. Look for mistakes in capitalization, punctuation, spelling, and simple past and present perfect verb forms. Then rewrite the essay correctly on the lines below.

The civil Rights Sacrifice

Just a few short decades ago, conditions for African americans in the united States are very unfair Today the situation have changed We owe these changes to the sacrifices of the people who where part of the Civil rights Movement.

Over the years, Both leaders and followers in the movement has helped to create change. Dr. Martin Luther king Jr. inspire many people to join the movement. these people included the Freedom Riders and those who took part in the lunch-counter sit-ins. They all helped end segrigation.

Yet being in the movement caused terrible losses. Dr. King give his life when he was assassinated in memphis. Through the years, many others has made sacrifices, too. They lost there jobs or got hurt physically during the struggle.

African Americans have enjoyd freedom for many years, thanks to the brave people who were willing to make sacrifices for this cause.

_____

_____

_____

_____

_____

_____

_____

_____

_____

_____

_____

SPELLING

Use after the spelling lesson.

Words with *cl, sl, st*
Some consonant letters stand for sounds that are **blended together**.

The letters **st** stand for the blended sound you hear at the beginning of the word *stained*.
The letters **sl** stand for the blended sound you hear at the beginning of the word *slate*.
The letters **cl** stand for the blended sound you hear at the beginning of the word *clear*.

Read the sentences from or about the selections. Find the incomplete word. Use the consonant blend *st, sl,* or *cl* to spell a word that makes sense in the sentence. Write the word in the space provided.

_____ **1.** But one hundred years later, we must face the tragic fact that the

Negro is __ill not free.

_____ **2.** Some of you have come from areas where your quest for freedom

left you battered by __orms of persecution. . . .

_____ **3.** . . . go back to the __ums and ghettos of our modern cities,

knowing that somehow this situation can and will be changed.

_____ **4.** I have a dream that . . . the sons of former __aves and the sons

of former slaveowners will be able to sit down together at a table of

brotherhood.

_____ **5.** With this faith we will be able to hew out of the mountain of despair

a __one of hope.

_____ **6.** When we let freedom ring, when we let it ring from every village and

every hamlet, from every __ate and every city, we will be able to

speed up that day when all of God's children . . . will be able to

join hands . . . .

_____ **7.** Lady Freedom wears a cap with feathers and __ars.

_____ **8.** Rita Dove saw the statue up close when it had been taken down to

be __eaned.

_____ **9.** What is __ung over one shoulder of Lady Freedom?

_____ **10.** Dr. King refers to the the De__aration of Independence.

UNIT 3 Voices of Freedom
PART 2

Contents

VOCABULARY

Use with textbook page 111.

Answer each question with a complete sentence. Use the word in *italics* in your answer.

1. I feel *disappointment* when a friend forgets my birthday. When have you felt

disappointment? _____

2. It is *fortunate* when someone is surprised with good news. What would make you

feel *fortunate?* _____

3. When I am lost, I feel worried and *tense*. What is something that makes you feel

tense? _____

4. Some people cannot *tolerate* loud noise. What do you find hard to *tolerate?*

_____

5. When he was accused of something he did not do, he felt *indignant* and upset. When

do you feel *indignant?* _____

Read the clues and complete the crossword puzzle. Use the words from the word box.

| fortunate | startling | tense | close |
| tolerate | steadily | group | fiercely |

ACROSS
2. strongly or extremely
4. surprising; unexpected

DOWN
1. put up with
2. having good luck
3. nervous and uptight

VOCABULARY BUILDING

Understanding *get* in Informal Usage

Get usually means "to receive or obtain," as in: *I get* a present. *I get* good grades.
However, *get* is often used informally and with different meanings in English. (The past simple form is *got*).

Here are some examples of different meanings of *get*.

get	Meaning	Example
get through	survive	I **got through** the test with good grades.
get	arrive somewhere	We usually **get** home very late.
get	understand something	He **got** the meaning of the book.
get into	become involved in	What's he **gotten** into?
get on with	continue	He **got on with** his reading.
get away with	is not caught	The crook **got away with** his crime.
get out of	be released, let go	I **get out of** school at three.
get up	step out of bed	I **got up** at dawn.
get around	move quickly	I really **get around** on my bike.

Read the sentences below. Write the meaning of the underlined phrase on the line. Use the chart above to help you.

1. The child really <u>gets around</u> on her tricycle. _____

2. Let's <u>get on with</u> the program.

_____

3. Unfortunately, the thief <u>got away with</u> the robbery.

_____

4. We'll <u>get through</u> the hard times.

_____

5. We <u>get out of</u> practice at 3:00.

_____

READING STRATEGY

Use with textbook page 111.

Visualizing means picturing something in your mind. Writers have many ways to help readers visualize.

- They often use adjectives and adverbs.
- They use colorful nouns and actions verbs.

Visualizing a story can help you form pictures of the characters, the action, and the setting.

Read the first column on page 113 and answer the questions.

1. In the first sentence, what adjective describes Miss Crocker's announcement? What do you think Miss Crocker does when she says this?

_____

_____

2. In the second paragraph, what action verb describes the student's reaction when they hear the announcement? How do you picture, or visualize the students when you read this word?

_____

_____

3. In the fifth paragraph, what do the words *beamed* and *proudly* tell you about Miss Crocker? How do you picture her? What does she look like?

_____

_____

4. In the sixth paragraph, what adjectives and adverbs describe the books? How do you picture their pages and covers?

_____

_____

_____

5. Now you have read several paragraphs of the story. In your own words, briefly tell how you picture Miss Crocker and her students as they receive the readers.

_____

_____

_____

Use with textbook pages 120–122.

Summary: "Words of Freedom"

This passage tells about three important American documents: The Declaration of Independence, the Constitution, and the Bill of Rights. The Declaration of Independence describes beliefs the American colonists held about freedom and equality, and proclaims that the American colonies would no longer be governed by the British. The Constitution describes the organization of the national government of the United States. The Bill of Rights describes the rights of each individual United States citizen.

Visual Summary

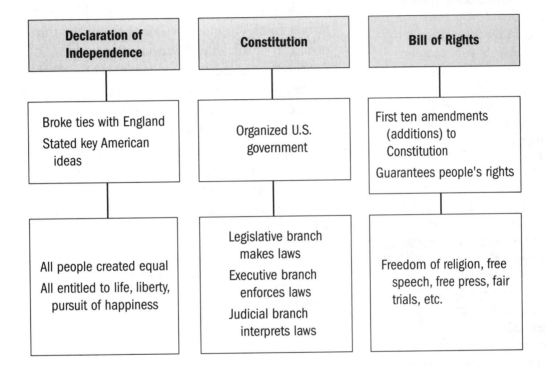

Declaration of Independence	Constitution	Bill of Rights
Broke ties with England Stated key American ideas	Organized U.S. government	First ten amendments (additions) to Constitution Guarantees people's rights
All people created equal All entitled to life, liberty, pursuit of happiness	Legislative branch makes laws Executive branch enforces laws Judicial branch interprets laws	Freedom of religion, free speech, free press, fair trials, etc.

Use What You Know

List three things you know about government.

1. _____

2. _____

3. _____

Text Structure: Informational Text

An informational text presents factual information to readers. Often it has headings that help you focus on important topics. Circle the heading on this page. What important topic do the paragraphs on this page cover?

_____

_____

MARK THE TEXT

Reading Strategy: Summarizing

Summarizing is retelling just the main ideas. In the first paragraph, underline the main purpose of the Declaration of Independence. Sum up the important information in the next two paragraphs.

MARK THE TEXT

_____

_____

_____

_____

_____

Words of Freedom

The Declaration of Independence (July 4, 1776)

By 1776, the American colonists realized that they needed to become independent from Great Britain. On July 4, the colonists broke all their ties with Britain. They formally announced their independence from Britain in the Declaration of Independence. The thirteen colonies immediately became thirteen American states. The main author of the Declaration of Independence was Thomas Jefferson, a lawyer and farmer from Virginia who later became the third president of the United States.

Two of the most important ideas expressed in the Declaration of Independence are that all people are "created equal" and that all people are entitled to "life, liberty, and the pursuit of happiness."

The belief in the equality of all people is central to the idea of democracy in the United States. The Declaration of Independence has inspired many people to fight for equality and to be tolerant of others.

_____

broke all their ties, ended their relationship with
pursuit, ability to have
democracy, a form of government in which citizens can vote to elect officials

Choose one and complete:
1. Draw your own chart showing each of the three branches of government, its head or chief, and its role or function.
2. Do research at the library or on the Internet to find out more about one of the documents mentioned in this article and its history. Take notes on what you find.
3. Create a collage that includes words from these documents along with photos and art that help illustrate the ideas in the documents.

The Constitution (1788)

After the United States won its independence from Britain, Americans faced a new challenge. The thirteen new states needed to find a way to work together as one country. Using principles from the Declaration of Independence, the Founding Fathers wrote the Constitution. This document forms the basis of the U.S. government.

The Constitution describes the organization of the national government. It divides the government into three parts, or branches:

- The legislative branch: This is the Congress. It makes the laws for the country.
- The executive branch: The president is the head, or chief, of this branch. It enforces laws made by Congress and controls the nation's military and foreign policy.
- The judicial branch: The Supreme Court is the head of this branch. The judicial branch interprets the laws that Congress passes and makes sure that the laws follow the principles of the Constitution.

---

principles, main beliefs or values
enforces, carries out; makes happen
interprets, explains what something, such as a document, means

Three Branches of Government

Legislative	Executive	Judicial
makes laws	enforces laws	interprets laws
Congress	President	Supreme Court
Senate ←→ House of Representatives	→ Vice President	

Comprehension Check

Underline the challenge that America faced after winning independence from Britain. How is that challenge related to the Constitution?

_____

_____

_____

MARK THE TEXT

Text Structure: Informational Text

Informational texts often include charts that help you understand important information. Circle the chart on this page. What three things does this chart help you understand?

MARK THE TEXT

1. _____

2. _____

3. _____

Reading Strategy: Summarizing

Underline the branches of government that you would include in a summary of the information on this page. Sum up the main information about each branch.

MARK THE TEXT

_____

_____

_____

_____

_____

_____

Comprehension Check

Underline the explanation of the system of checks and balances. Why do you think the Founding Fathers wanted to be sure that no one branch of government had more power than another?

MARK THE TEXT

_____

_____

_____

_____

Text Structure: Informational Text

Informational texts often define or explain key terms. Find the second sentence under the heading "The Bill of Rights." Underline the key term, draw an arrow to the word that explains it, and circle that word.

MARK THE TEXT

Reading Strategy: Summarizing

Underline the examples of rights that the Bill of Rights guarantees. Based on these examples, sum up what the Bill of Rights does.

MARK THE TEXT

_____

_____

_____

The Founding Fathers wanted to be certain that no one branch of government had more power than another. They established what is called the system of checks and balances. Each branch of government has some—but not total—power over the other two branches. In 1788, the Constitution of the United States became law, and in 1789, George Washington was elected the first president of the United States.

The Bill of Rights (1791)

Many citizens were concerned that the Constitution created a strong national government, but did not protect the basic rights of people. As a result, ten amendments, or additions, were added to the Constitution. These amendments are called the Bill of Rights.

The Bill of Rights guarantees personal rights such as freedom of religion, freedom of speech, freedom of the press, and a fair trial in court. The rights in the Bill of Rights form the foundation of American democracy. This was the first time that a country wrote a constitution that promised to protect the individual civil and political rights of all its free citizens.

---

guarantees, promises
foundation, basis; the most important part
civil, of the government, state, or nation
political, relating to the government or politics of a country
rights, freedoms and advantages that people have

Retell It!

Original copies of the three documents (The Charters of Freedom) that you read about are at the National Archives and Records Administration (NARA) Exhibit Hall in Washington, D.C. Imagine that you are a tour guide there, telling visitors about the documents. Write what you might say about each document. Use the Internet to find out more about NARA and The Charters of Freedom.

_____

_____

_____

_____

_____

_____

_____

_____

_____

_____

Reader's Response

What did this article help you appreciate about the three documents?

_____

_____

_____

_____

_____

Think About the Skill

How did summarizing help you better understand the information in this article?

_____

_____

_____

GRAMMAR

Use with textbook page 124.

Gerunds and Infinitives

Gerunds and infinitives are verbs that act like nouns. Gerunds are formed by using the base form of a verb + *ing*. Some verbs, like *swimming*, double the final consonant before adding *-ing*. Infinitives are formed by using *to* + the base form of the verb.

They love **running**.   They love **to run**.

Some verbs can be followed by a gerund or an infinitive: *begin, love, like, hate, prefer*.

We like **singing** in the morning.   We like **to sing** in the morning.

Some verbs can only be followed by a gerund: *enjoy, quit, finish, suggest, keep*.

I quit **playing** the flute last year.   I enjoy **swimming**.

Some verbs can only be followed by an infinitive: *hope, plan, need, want, ask*.

We asked **to see** the librarian.   We wanted **to go** to the library.

Circle the gerund or infinitive in parentheses that completes the sentences. In some sentences, both choices are correct. Circle both.

1. We promise (to take / taking) good care of our new books.

2. I noticed the first graders anxiously (to watch / watching) the disappearing pile.

3. I began (to browse / browsing) through the spotted pages.

4. I began (to read / reading) while Miss Crocker's voice droned on monotonously.

5. Miss Crocker continued (to beam / beaming) as she called each fourth grader to her desk.

6. Little Man raised his head and continued (to look / looking) into her eyes.

7. Cassie wanted (to return / returning) her book, too.

8. Cassie offered (to explain / explaining) why Little Man did what he did.

9. Cassie needed (to tell / telling) Miss Crocker something, but Miss Crocker did not understand.

10. Little Man did not want (to pick up / picking up) the book.

GRAMMAR

Use after the lesson on past progressive verb forms.

Past Progressive

The **past progressive** is a verb form that includes *was/wasn't* or *were/weren't* + the *-ing* form of the verb. This verb phrase describes an action that was in progress in the past.

Miss Crocker *was teaching* the class.
Cassie *was reading* the old book.
Cassie and Little Man *were watching* each other.
Little Man *wasn't smiling*.
We *weren't getting* new books.

Complete each sentence with the past progressive form of the verb in parentheses.

1. Cassie _____ at the reader. (look)

2. The students _____ to Miss Crocker. (listen)

3. Little Man _____ by the age of four. (read)

4. Miss Crocker _____ out the books. (give)

5. The books _____ in a pile on the desk. (sit)

Use each past progressive verb in a sentence that tells about what happened in the selection.

6. was beaming _____

7. was stomping _____

8. was holding _____

9. was browsing _____

10. was asking _____

SKILLS FOR WRITING

Use with textbook page 125.

Writing a Poem

When you write a poem, you use words in an interesting way to create sounds, images, and rhythms.

Look at Rita Dove's poem on pages 103 and 104 of your textbook. Answer the questions.

1. What is this poem about?

_____

_____

_____

2. How is the poem different from a nonfiction article or an essay? How is it different from a short story?

_____

_____

_____

3. Read the third stanza on page 103. What words does the poet use to create images of the statue?

_____

_____

_____

4. Read the fourth stanza on page 103. How does the poet describe the statue?

_____

_____

_____

5. Read the first two lines of the second stanza on page 104. What word is repeated to create a rhythm?

_____

_____

_____

PROOFREADING AND EDITING

Use with textbook page 126.

Read the poem below carefully. Find all the mistakes. Look for mistakes in capitalization, punctuation, and use of gerunds and infinitives. Then rewrite the poem correctly on the lines below.

Peace

Everyone hopes to finding peace.

Everyon wants violence to cease.

Let angar and bitterness fade away.

Let the calm of morning arive and stay.

This may be a dreem that never ends.

Still, i hope, one day w'ell all be friends.

I will never stop to hope, I am sure.

Indeed, we all want seeing piece forevermore.

_____

_____

_____

_____

_____

_____

_____

_____

_____

_____

_____

_____

_____

_____

SPELLING

Use after the spelling lesson.

Spelling words with *sh-*, and *th-*

Consonant digraphs are two-letters that stand for one sound. Review the sounds of the
following digraphs by reading these examples aloud.

sh	th (voiced)	th (unvoiced)
shook	that	thing
she	another	thank

Read the sentences from or about the selection *Roll of Thunder, Hear My Cry*. Find the
incomplete word. Use the correct digraph to spell the word in the space provided.

_____ **1.** Each four__ grader was called to Miss Crocker's desk.

_____ **2.** Cassie did not want to __ink of Little Man's disappointment when he
saw the books as they really were.

_____ **3.** Little Man was pu__ing a book back upon the desk.

_____ **4.** Miss Crocker told him, "Now you take that book or get no__ing at
all!"

_____ **5.** __en his eyes grew wide,

_____ **6.** Miss Crocker ru__ed to Little Man and grabbed him up in powerful
hands.

_____ **7.** Cassie __ook her head, realizing Miss Crocker didn't know what she
was talking about.

_____ **8.** He just stood staring down at the open book, __ivering with
indignant anger.

_____ **9.** "S-see what __ey called us," I said, afraid she had not seen.

_____ **10.** "__at's what you are," she said coldly. "Now go sit down."

UNIT 4 Risks and Challenges

PART 1

Contents

VOCABULARY

Use with textbook page 137.

Read each sentence. Choose the best meaning for the underlined word by circling the letter.

1. Fugitive slaves were always worried about being caught.

    a. free   b. runaway   c. confident   d. rich

2. The healthcare workers worked together to create a network.

    a. salary   b. restaurant   c. system   d. uniform

3. We adopted our cat at the local animal shelter.

    a. safe place   b. hotel   c. countryside   d. school

4. Many of the spirituals sung by slaves are still sung in churches today.

    a. marches   b. religious songs   c. poems   d. chorus

5. Learn about African American culture and heritage at the Folk Art Museum.

    a. traditions   b. industry   c. geography   d. information

Read the clues. Use the words in the box to complete the crossword puzzle. (Hint: You will not use all the words.)

| heritage | shelter | freedom | operate |
| spirituals | runaway | railroad | network |

ACROSS
2. songs sung by slaves
3. a set of contacts
4. culture and traditions

DOWN
1. escaping
2. a safe, protected place

VOCABULARY BUILDING

Compound Words

Compound words are formed by combining two or more words. Usually, the two words make one new word with a new meaning. Sometimes, the words are not joined, but are next to each other. The two words, taken together, have a new meaning. Draw a line from the word in column A to the word in Column B that makes a compound word. Then write the compound word in the space provided. Use a dictionary if you need to.

Column A	Column B	Compound Word
1. under	worker	_____
2. run	times	_____
3. rail	spread	_____
4. station	holder	_____
5. black	road	_____
6. day	master	_____
7. slave	outs	_____
8. some	light	_____
9. field	away	_____
10. wide	ground	_____

READING STRATEGY

Use with textbook page 137.

Skimming for Main Ideas

After previewing a text, good readers **skim** it to find the **main ideas**. Here are the steps to follow:

- Read the text quickly to find the main ideas.
- Look for the main ideas in each paragraph. A main idea is often the first sentence in the paragraph.
- When you are done, see if you can summarize what the text is mainly about.
- Then go back and read for details.

Skim the two paragraphs under the heading "Risk Takers" on pages 138 and 139. Then answer the questions to help you find the main ideas.

1. Paragraph 1: What risks did runaway slaves take?

_____

_____

2. Paragraph 2: Who were the other people who took risks?

_____

_____

Now go back and reread the two paragraphs more carefully. Answer the questions to help you find some details.

3. Paragraph 1: What happened to slaves if they were caught?

_____

_____

4. Paragraph 1: What happened to them even if they were not caught?

_____

_____

5. Paragraph 2: Why did people take risks to help runaway slaves?

_____

_____

_____

Use with textbook pages 146–148.

Summary: "Five New Words at a Time"

In this article, Yu-Lan, a Chinese girl who has moved to the United States, tells about her trouble learning English. No one in her family speaks English, and school is so crowded Yu-Lan cannot learn there. Although Yu-Lan's mother works hard at her job, she takes time to study English with her daughter. Together, the two of them learn five new words every day. Yu-Lan admires her mother's strength, and they both learn English quickly.

Visual Summary

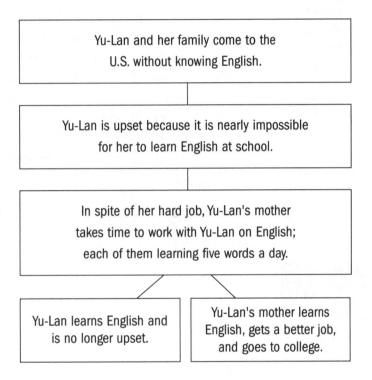

Yu-Lan and her family come to the U.S. without knowing English.

Yu-Lan is upset because it is nearly impossible for her to learn English at school.

In spite of her hard job, Yu-Lan's mother takes time to work with Yu-Lan on English; each of them learning five words a day.

Yu-Lan learns English and is no longer upset.

Yu-Lan's mother learns English, gets a better job, and goes to college.

Use What You Know

List one challenge you have learning English as a second language.

_____

_____

_____

Text Structure: Personal Narrative

In a personal narrative, someone tells about events in his or her own life. This person is called the narrator. Circle the name of the narrator of this selection. What do you learn about her background in the opening sentence?

MARK THE TEXT

_____

_____

_____

Reading Strategy: Identifying with a Character

To identify with a character, consider what you have in common with him or her. Underline the writer's feelings about going to school each morning. Can you identify with the writer? Why or why not?

MARK THE TEXT

_____

_____

_____

_____

_____

Five New Words at a Time

Yu-Lan (Mary) Ying

My family came to America in 1985. No one spoke a word of English. In school, I was in an English as a Second Language class with other foreign-born children. My class was so overcrowded that it was impossible for the teacher to teach English properly. I dreaded going to school each morning because of the fear of not understanding what people were saying and the fear of being laughed at.

At that time, my mother, Tai-Chih, worked part time in a Chinese restaurant from late afternoon till late in the night. It was her unfamiliarity with the English language that forced her to work in a Chinese-speaking environment. Although her job exhausted her, my mother still woke up early in the morning to cook breakfast for my brother and me. Like a hen guarding her chicks, she never neglected us because of her fatigue.

---

dreaded, was afraid of; feared
neglected, did not take care of
fatigue, tiredness; exhaustion

"Five New Words at a Time" by Yu-Lan (Mary) Ying, originally published in *The New York Times*, March 6, 1993. Reprinted by permission of *The New York Times*.

So it was not surprising that very soon my mother noticed something was troubling me. When I said nothing was wrong, my mother answered, "You are my daughter. When something is bothering you, I feel it too." The pain and care in her moon-shaped eyes made me burst into the tears I had held back for so long. I explained to her the fear I had of going to school. "Learning English is not impossible," my mother said. She cheerfully suggested that the two of us work together to learn the language at home with books. The **confidence** and **determination** my mother had were **admirable** because English was as new to her as it was to me.

That afternoon I saw my mother in a different light as she waited for me by the school fence. Although she was the shortest of all the mothers there, her face with her welcoming smile and big, black eyes was the most promising. The afternoon sun shone brightly on her long, black hair creating an **aura** that distinguished her from others.

My mother and I immediately began reading together and memorizing five new words a day. My mother with her encouraging attitude made the routine fun and interesting. The fact that she was sacrificing her resting time before going to work so that I could learn English made me see the strength she possessed. It made me admire my mother even more.

_____

confidence, belief in yourself
determination, strong desire to do something; resolve
admirable, worthy; deserving respect
aura, light that seems to come from a person

Reading Strategy: Identifying with a Character

Circle the words that tell why Yu-Lan burst into tears. What does this show about how close she and her mother are? Have you ever felt this kind of closeness with a family member?

Text Structure: Personal Narrative

In a personal narrative, the narrator uses first-person pronouns such as *I, me*, and *my* to talk about himself or herself. Underline three first-person pronouns the narrator uses in the last paragraph. When the narrator uses *she* or *her*, which character is she talking about?

Comprehension Check

Circle what the mother was sacrificing. Why was this a sacrifice?

Comprehension Check

Underline the name of the exam the mother was able to pass after she learned English. What has the mother apparently done as a result of learning English?

MARK THE TEXT

_____

_____

Text Structure: Personal Narrative

The narrator in a personal narrative often looks back on experiences that happened a while ago. Circle the number of years that passed since the reading experience the narrator described. About how old do you think the narrator was when she and her mother began learning five new words a day? Why?

MARK THE TEXT

_____

_____

_____

_____

Reading Strategy: Identifying with a Character

Underline what the narrator calls her mother in the last sentence. Can you identify with the narrator's feelings about her mother? Why or why not?

MARK THE TEXT

_____

_____

_____

_____

Very soon, I began to comprehend what everyone was saying and people could understand me. The person solely responsible for my accomplishment and happiness was my mother. The reading also helped my mother learn English so that she was able to pass the postal entrance exam.

It has been seven years since that reading experience with my mother. She is now forty-three and in her second year at college. My brother and I have a strong sense of who we are because of the strong values my mother established for herself and her children. My admiration and gratitude for her are endless. That is why my mother is truly the guiding light of my life.

_____

gratitude, thankfulness; appreciation

Choose one and complete:

1. Draw a picture of an event in the selection.
2. Using the Internet or another up-to-date source, find out more about immigration to the United States in the 1980s, when the author came to the United States. Make a map or chart showing how many people came and from what countries or regions.
3. Apply the "five new words a day" rule to your own life. List the words and their meanings in a journal. Begin with five words from this selection.

Retell It!

Imagine you are retelling the selection from the mother's point of view. List the experiences and feelings you would include.

_____

_____

_____

_____

_____

_____

_____

_____

_____

Reader's Response

What did you think of the five-new-words-a-day method of learning English? Why?

_____

_____

_____

_____

_____

Think About the Skill

How did identifying with the narrator help you better understand the selection?

_____

_____

_____

_____

GRAMMAR

Use with textbook page 150.

Prepositions and Prepositional Phrases

Prepositions are words that tell *where, in what direction,* and *when.*

where:	**at, in, by**
in what direction:	**down, across, to, toward, at**
when:	**before, in, after**

A **prepositional phrase** includes a preposition (P) and an object (O).

  P O   P   O

at <u>school</u>   **in** <u>a Chinese restaurant</u>

Read each sentence. Circle the preposition and underline the object.

1. She waited by the river.

2. She ran away to Philadelphia.

3. The runaway slaves stayed in a safe house.

4. Harriet Tubman ran away before sunrise.

5. They traveled across the river.

Write sentences that use prepositional phrases to answer these questions. Then underline the preposition and its object. Remember to write complete sentences. Follow the example.

Example: *When* did the Underground Railroad exist?
              It existed <u>in the nineteenth century</u>.

6. *Where* did slaves look for shelter on the Underground Railroad?

    _____

7. *When* did Harriet Tubman escape?

    _____

8. *In what direction* did runaway slaves usually travel?

    _____

9. *Where* did the Underground Railroad operate?

    _____

10. *When* did most of the slaves travel?

    _____

GRAMMAR

Use after the lesson on prepositional phrases with time.

Prepositional Phrases with Time

Prepositional phrases can indicate **when** something is happening or happened. A prepositional phrase must include a preposition and an object. It may also include adjectives or other words.

We came to America <u>in 1985</u>.
We arrived <u>during a rainy spring</u>.
<u>For the first few weeks</u>, the rain did not stop.

Use these prepositions to talk about time.

about	after	around	at	before	
beyond	by	during	for	from	in
on	over	since	until	throughout	

Circle the preposition that best completes each sentence.

Example: ((Throughout)/ Beyond) the rest of her life, Harriet suffered from blackouts.

1. (At / Over) that time, slavery was more widespread in the South.

2. (In / On) the mid-1800s, slavery was illegal in the northern states.

3. (During / Since) this period, it was still legal in the South.

4. (For / Until) many years, slaves escaped to the North.

5. Slavery continued (for / in) many years in the South.

SKILLS FOR WRITING

Use with textbook page 151.

Writing Interview Questions and Responses

Before you do an interview, you need to write questions. Use **wh-questions** that begin with the words *who, what, where, when, why* and the word *how*.

Imagine you could interview Harriet Tubman. Write five questions that you would like to ask her. Read the hints in parentheses ( ) to help you.

1. (her childhood) _____

_____

_____

_____

2. (reason she ran away) _____

_____

_____

_____

3. (after she reached freedom) _____

_____

_____

4. (helping others) _____

_____

_____

5. (feelings about her accomplishments) _____

_____

_____

PROOFREADING AND EDITING

Use with textbook page 152.

Read the summary sentence and the interview carefully. Look for mistakes in capitalization, punctuation, verb tense, and the use of prepositions and prepositional phrases. Then rewrite the interview correctly on the lines below.

In this interview, i asked Yu-Lan about her most challenging experience.

Me: What was the most challenging experience you ever had

Yu-Lan: It was getting used to my new life here with the united States.

Me: Where did you come from? When did you move at the United States?

Yu-Lan: I move here from Shanghai, china. My family came here on 1985.

Me: Why was getting used to life here such a challenge.

Yu-lan: I can give you many reasons: getting used at a new language, a new culture, and a new school. I barely speak English when I got here For a while, it was really tough.

Me: How long had you studied English on school during you arrived here

Yu-Lan: I hadnt studied it at all. I study Japanese across five years. I think Ill be studying English on the rest in my life!

_____

_____

_____

_____

_____

_____

_____

_____

_____

_____

_____

_____

Name _____ Date _____

SPELLING

Use after the spelling lesson.

Doubling Final Consonant and Adding -ing

Verbs that end in a short vowel followed by one consonant usually double the final consonant before adding -ing.

run + ing	running	stop + ing	stopping
begin + ing	beginning	admit + ing	admitting

Most other verbs just add -ing.

know + ing	knowing	sleep + ing	sleeping
try + ing	trying	rest + ing	resting

Add -ing to each verb. Write the new form of the verb on the line.

1. think _____

2. follow _____

3. scamper _____

4. win _____

5. hunt _____

Read each sentence. Circle the word with -ing that is spelled incorrectly. Write it correctly on the line.

6   Runing away on the Underground

Railroad was dangerous. _____

7. In the begining, slaves had to escape from the slaveholders. _____

8. Runaways found their way by followwing the North Star. _____

9. Geting caught was always a possibility. _____

10. Stoping to rest was necessary but dangerous. _____

UNIT 4 Risks and Challenges

PART 2

Contents

VOCABULARY

Use with textbook page 155.

Write a sentence to answer each question. Use the underlined word in your answer.

1. When people feel awkward, they feel uncomfortable. How can you help an awkward person feel comfortable?

_____

2. Light is essential for plant growth. Without light, plants will die. What is something else that is essential for plants to grow?

_____

3. A lion is an animal that roars and acts ferociously. What other animal can act ferociously?

_____

4. Something that is invisible cannot be seen. What is something that is invisible?

_____

5. Some wild animals can be tamed, so they won't hurt people. What wild animals do you know about that have been tamed?

_____

Read the clues. Use words from the box to complete the crossword puzzle.

clever	disturbing	awkward	invisible	tamed
hunter	dangerous	essential	monotonous	unique

ACROSS
1. the only one of its kind
4. boring
5. uncomfortable or embarrassing

DOWN
2. necessary
3. made less wild

VOCABULARY BUILDING

Understanding Synonyms

A **synonym** is a word that has the same or nearly the same meaning as another word. A word can have more than one synonym. To find synonyms, use a thesaurus, a dictionary, or the synonym finder on your computer.

Word	Synonym
essential	necessary
dangerous	perilous
monotonous	boring
remember	recall
unique	uncommon

Synonyms provide you with choices when you write or speak. They can also help you find just the right words to make your meaning clear. Using synonyms makes your writing more interesting and descriptive.

Complete each sentence. Choose a synonym from the box that means the same as the word in parentheses ( ).

1. The fox tells the Little Prince that what is (essential) _____ cannot be seen.

2. The fox says the Little Prince doesn't look (dangerous) _____ because he is little.

3. Life is (monotonous) _____ when everything is always the same.

4. The fox tells the Little Prince that he will always (remember)

_____ him when he sees the wheatfields.

5. A talking fox is certainly (unique) _____ .

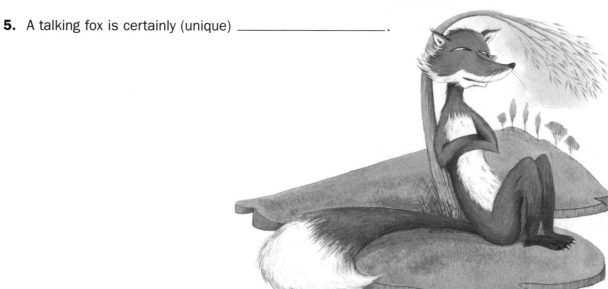

READING STRATEGY

Use with textbook page 155.

Using Text Structure

Different kinds of texts—plays, stories, and poems—have different kinds of text structures. Knowing these structures can help you better understand what you read.

	Plays	**Stories**
Characters	Characters' names appear at the beginning of a line, usually followed by a colon. In most plays, a list of characters appears at the beginning of the play.	Characters' names appear in the running text.
Dialogue	What a character says appears after the colon that follows the character's name.	What a character says appears in the text and is set off with quotation marks.
Characters' Feelings and Actions	How a character feels and/or acts is often found in the stage directions, which usually appear in parentheses.	How a character feels and/or acts is found in the text.
Setting	The setting is usually described in the stage directions.	The setting is described or revealed in the text.

Preview the text on pages 156 and 157. Use what you noticed about the text structure and the chart above to answer the questions.

1. Is this reading selection a play or a story? How can you tell?

_____

_____

2. Who are the characters? How can you tell?

_____

3. How do you know what the characters are feeling?

_____

4. What part of the text tells you what the characters are doing?

_____

5. How is dialogue shown in this text?

_____

Use with textbook pages 166–168.

Summary: "Performance Anxiety"

This article tells about the stress many people feel when they have to speak or perform in front of others. It describes what happens to the body when a person feels this way. It lists steps to take if you feel nervous about speaking or performing.

Visual Summary

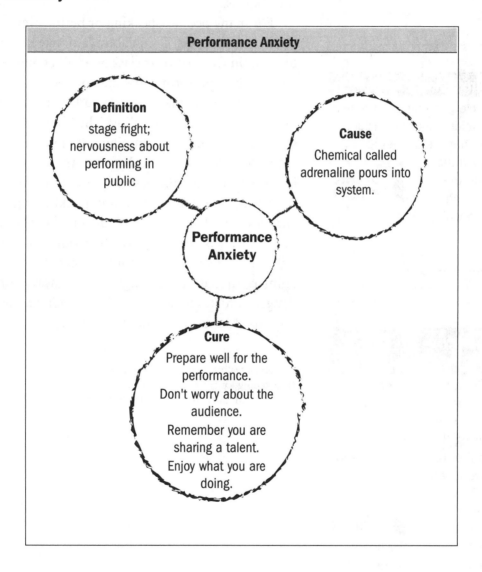

Performance Anxiety

Definition
stage fright; nervousness about performing in public

Cause
Chemical called adrenaline pours into system.

Performance Anxiety

Cure
Prepare well for the performance.
Don't worry about the audience.
Remember you are sharing a talent.
Enjoy what you are doing.

Performance Anxiety

Use What You Know

Describe how you feel when you take a test or speak in front of an audience.

_____

_____

_____

Text Structure: Science Article

A science article presents information on a topic in science. It may include special terms that are defined or explained. Circle the term defined in the first sentence, and underline its meaning. What is a "stressor"?

MARK THE TEXT

_____

_____

Reading Strategy: Skimming for Main Ideas

When you skim a text, you read it quickly to find the main ideas. You can then read it more slowly and carefully, noticing the supporting details. Skim the third paragraph and look for the word "adrenaline." Underline it. Read more slowly. Did you circle the word *adrenaline* the first time it was used? What is adrenaline, and when does the body release it into the bloodstream?

MARK THE TEXT

_____

_____

_____

Stress is the reaction of your mind and body to situations that seem dangerous or disturbing. A "stressor" is something that causes this reaction. There are many kinds of stressors. A test in school, an argument, a threatening situation, or an injury might cause stress.

For many people, speaking or performing in public causes stress. Think about a time when you had to stand in front of your class or another audience, and speak or perform. How did you feel?

If you are like many of us, you felt stress. There are physical causes for this feeling. The body responds to stressful situations by pumping a chemical called adrenaline into your bloodstream. Adrenaline increases your heartbeat, giving you more energy and preparing your body to respond quickly. These changes are often called the "fight-or-flight" response, because they prepare you to either run or stay and fight the stressor. This response is present in all animals, so that they can fight or run away from danger. Athletes today use their own adrenaline response to run faster and play better.

---

anxiety, a feeling of worry or nervousness
threatening, causing fear or alarm
injury, a cut, burn, or other harm to the body

Today, most of our stressors are not things we fight or run away from. Actors don't run off the stage or stay to fight with the audience! But our bodies still react to stress. We release adrenaline. Our breathing and heartbeat are faster. Our hands feel cold as blood is pumped away from these areas to other places. And less blood flows to our digestive system. We might feel "butterflies" in our stomach when we are frightened or nervous.

In modern life, these feelings are not always good or useful. Luckily, there are ways to reduce them. In the case of performance anxiety, or "stage fright"—a term taken from the theater—there are other specific things you can do to reduce stress. Breathing deeply can help relax you. This will help your flow of blood and oxygen return to normal. Here are some other tips you can use to calm your mind and body before a performance.

1. **First of all, prepare.** You will be more relaxed if you feel ready. If you are giving a speech, practice in front of a mirror. Practice on tape. Give the speech to your dog, cat, or baby sister. It helps to practice in front of a small audience before you face a large one. It's also helpful to practice your lines with friends or family members. If you are singing or playing a musical instrument, perform your piece for friends or family. And remember that it's important to come to all the play or concert rehearsals.

_____

release, let circulate in our bodies

digestive system, the mouth, stomach, intestines, and other organs that help people or animals eat, process food, and get rid of waste

---

Reading Strategy: Skimming for Main Ideas

Skim the first paragraph on this page. What is the paragraph's main idea?

_____

_____

_____

_____

Comprehension Check

Underline three things that happen to the body when adrenaline is released. Why do you think this reaction was once useful? Why is it not useful in modern life?

MARK THE TEXT

_____

_____

_____

_____

_____

Text Structure: Science Article

Science articles often include tips or steps in numbered lists. Circle the number and boldfaced words that follow it on this page. Read the sentence that introduces the list. Underline the words that tell what the list will provide. What tip or advice in the second paragraph on this page could have been part of the numbered list?

MARK THE TEXT

_____

Text Structure: Science Article

The text on this page continues the numbered list. Underline the headings in bold-faced type. How many items are there in the numbered list in this article?

_____

_____

Comprehension Check

Circle the two examples that support the second tip. In general, what does item 2 tell performers not to assume about the audience?

_____

_____

_____

Reading Strategy: Skimming for Main Ideas

Skim the last item in the numbered list. What does this tip tell performers to do about mistakes they make?

_____

_____

_____

_____

2. **Don't try to guess what your audience is thinking.** If you see a man with his eyes closed, for example, don't **immediately** think that he is bored. Maybe he is listening and concentrating. Or if you hear people talking, don't **assume** it's because they are not happy with your performance. Maybe they are asking questions about the piece you are performing.

3. **Remember that you have a talent and that you are sharing it.** Think of your audience as wanting to receive what you have to give. Think of your performance as a gift from you to your listeners, and do your best. Try looking at different people in the audience and image that you are performing just for them. Make eye contact. Speak to them. Sing to them. Play for them.

4. **Allow yourself to enjoy what you are doing!** Feel your emotions, and enjoy the excitement of your performance. Don't let mistakes **interfere** with your enjoyment. If you forgive your own mistakes and keep going when you make them, the audience will probably forgive them, too! Often an audience doesn't care as much about **perfection** as about the feeling the performer can **project**. If you make a mistake, forget it, keep going, and keep your heart in your performance!

_____

immediately, right away; without waiting
assume, believe that something it true
interfere, interrupt, stop, or get in the way of
perfection, faultlessness; excellence
project, communicate with the audience

Choose one and complete:
1. Create a painting, drawing, or collage that you think expresses the feelings of someone with performance anxiety.
2. Find out more about performance anxiety by researching it on the Internet. Take notes.
3. Choose music that you think could help calm someone down before a performance. Describe the music, and tape it.

Retell It!

Imagine that you will interview a performer who will use information from the article to answer your questions. List two or three key questions you will ask. Then list the answers.

_____

_____

_____

_____

_____

_____

_____

_____

_____

Reader's Response

How did this article help you understand your own reactions to stress?

_____

_____

_____

_____

_____

_____

_____

Think About the Skill

How did skimming for main ideas help you better understand the article?

_____

_____

_____

_____

GRAMMAR

Use with textbook page 170.

Contractions and Apostrophes

A **contraction** is two words combined into one. Some letters are left out. An **apostrophe** (') takes the place of the missing letters.

He **was not** afraid.   He **wasn't** afraid.

Read the sentences. Circle the contraction for the underlined words. Use the common contractions listed on page 170 of your textbook if you need help.

1. You <u>do not</u> live around here. (do'nt / don't / doesn't)

2. If you could tame me, <u>you would</u> be unique. (youd / you're/ you'd)

3. <u>It is</u> a ritual. (its / it's / 'ts)

4. <u>I am</u> right here under the apple tree. (Im / I'm / I'am)

5. <u>I will</u> be very excited. (ll'I / I'll / Ill)

Read the sentences. Write the contraction for the underlined words.

6. You <u>are not</u> like my rose.

_____

7. To me, <u>you are</u> just another boy.

_____

8. I <u>do not</u> think that is right.

_____

9. <u>I have</u> had a lot of practice.

_____

10. You <u>do not</u> talk like my rose.

_____

GRAMMAR

Possessives

Use after the lesson about possessives.

A **possessive** shows that something belongs to someone or something. Use an apostrophe (') and s to form most possessives. Here are the rules for forming possessives.

- Singular noun: Add an apostrophe and s:
  the rose that belongs to the boy   the **boy's** rose

- Plural nouns: If the noun ends in s, just add an apostrophe.
  the books that belong to the girls   the **girls'** books

- Plural nouns: If the noun does not end in s, add an apostrophe and s.
  the dreams of the children   the **children's** dreams

Rewrite each phrase as a possessive.

Example: the plane that belongs to the pilot   _the pilot's plane_

1. the guns that belong to the hunters _____

2. the friend of the Little Prince _____

3. the rose that belongs to the Little Prince _____

4. the words of the fox _____

5. the ideas that belong to the men _____

SKILLS FOR WRITING

Use with textbook page 171.

Writing Dialogue

Stories and personal narratives often have **dialogue**. To show dialogue, the writer:

- places **quotation marks** (" ") before and after the exact words of a speaker.
- uses a capital letter at the beginning of the words.
- ends with a comma, a period, a question mark, or an exclamation point. The punctuation goes inside the closing quotation mark.

> "Who are you?" asked Little Prince.
> "I'm a fox," said the animal.
> The boy smiled and said, "Will you come play with me?"
> "Play with you?" said the Fox. "I can't play with you."

Rewrite the following dialogue with the correct punctuation. Use the rules and examples above to help you.

1. I wish you would leave my chickens alone said the farmer.

_____

_____

2. The fox answered I think chickens are wonderful birds!

_____

_____

3. Please leave my henhouse yelled the farmer.

_____

_____

4. The fox laughed and said I will do anything you want.

_____

_____

5. Thank you said the farmer. Maybe we can be friends now.

_____

_____

PROOFREADING AND EDITING

Use with textbook page 172.

Read the dialogue below carefully. Look for mistakes in capitalization, punctuation, and the use of contractions. Find all the mistakes. Then rewrite the dialogue correctly on the lines below.

"Maria, dont be nervous about dancing tonight, I said"

"Im not stressed, she answered. "Iv'e been practicing in front of the mirror at three weeks.

"Remember to make eye contact about your audience" I told her. Youv'e got talent and youre going to be great

Maria smiled and said Il'l enjoy myself tonight You'wll see.

_____

_____

_____

_____

_____

_____

_____

_____

_____

_____

_____

_____

_____

_____

SPELLING

Use after the spelling lesson.

Spelling Words with s, sh, and z

The consonant letters s and z can sometimes stand for the same sound. The consonant letter s and the digraph sh can also stand for the same sound. Other times, s stands for the sound heard at the beginning of the work *sit*.

Read the following sentences and decide which letter or digraph to use. Hint: one word uses z or s twice. Use a dictionary if you need help. Write the word in the space provided.

_____   **1.** But how can i be __ure it's not a trap.

_____   **2.** You're one of tho__e hunters.

_____   **3.** They have gun__ and they hunt.

_____   **4.** FOX nu__les like a puppy dog as lights fade.

_____   **5.** Oh, but this wa__n't on Earth.

_____   **6.** FOX: No. (Pau__e.)

_____   **7.** __all we begin?

_____   **8.** Let's play hide and __eek.

_____   **9.** You are not as all like my ro__e.

_____   **10.** What is essential is invi__ible to the eye.

UNIT 5 Reach for the Stars

PART 1

Contents

VOCABULARY

Use with textbook page 183.

Read each definition. Then use the underlined word in a sentence.

Example: A meteorite is a piece of rock or metal that travels through space and enters the Earth's atmosphere.

We saw a crater that was made by a giant meteorite.

1. Comets are bright heavenly bodies with a long tail of light. Comets travel around the sun. _____

2. When an animal is extinct, it no longer exists.

   _____

3. A gas is a state of matter. It is not liquid or solid.

   _____

4. An asteroid is a rocky or metallic object that travels around the sun.

   _____

5. Gravity is the force that pulls objects toward the center of the Earth.

   _____

Read the clues. Use the words in the box to complete the crossword puzzle.

| meteorite | gas | extinct | gravity | comet |

ACROSS
2. having died out
5. force that pulls things toward Earth so that they won't float away into space

DOWN
1. a remaining piece of rock or metal that enters Earth's atmosphere
3. heavenly bodies with a glowing tail of light
4. an air like substance

VOCABULARY BUILDING

Understanding Antonyms

Antonyms are words that have the opposite or nearly the opposite meanings. To find antonyms, look in a thesaurus or dictionary. Read the words and their antonyms in the chart below.

Words	Antonyms
tiny, small	huge, enormous, large
warm	cool
close, near	far, distant
all	none
night	day

Complete each sentence with an antonym from the chart for each underlined word.

1. The stars look <u>tiny</u>, but with a telescope they appear _____.

2. The moon seems so <u>close</u> to Earth, but it is really very _____ from it.

3. During the _____, the sun moves across the sky, but at <u>night</u> it drops below the horizon.

4. <u>All</u> the planets reflect light from the sun, however, _____ of the planets glow.

5. Planets close to the sun are very <u>warm</u>, and those that are faraway are very

_____.

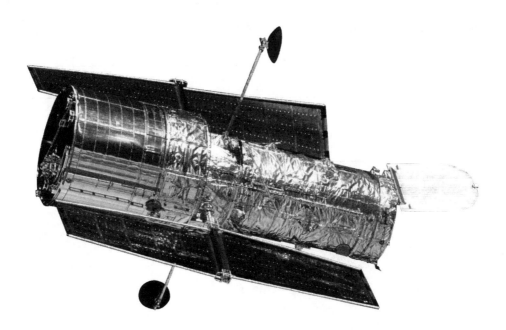

READING STRATEGY

Use with textbook page 183.

Using a *K-W-L-H* Chart

Using a *K-W-L-H* chart can help you read difficult texts. It can help you set a purpose for reading. It can also help you remember information.

Follow these steps to fill out the chart:

First, fill out columns *K* and *W* on the chart.

- Write **what you already know** about the solar system in the first column.
- Write questions about **what you want to know** in the second column.

Next, read the title and first three paragraphs of the article on pages 184 and 185 in your textbook. Then complete columns *L* and *H* on the chart.

- Record **what you learned** in the third column.
- Record **how you learned** the new information in the last column.

Topic: Solar System

K–What I Already Know	W–What I Want to Know	L–What I Learned	H–How I Learned
1.	2.	3.	4.

5. What is your purpose for reading this article? _____

_____

_____

_____

_____

Use with textbook pages 194–196.

Summary: "On van Gogh's *Starry Night*" and "Escape at Bedtime"

The first poem gives the speaker's impressions of van Gogh's famous painting, which shows a night sky full of clouds and bright stars. "Escape at Bedtime" describes the night sky as seen through the eyes of a child.

Visual Summary

"On van Gogh's *Starry Night*"	"Escape at Bedtime"
• describes van Gogh's famous painting *Starry Night* • indicates the painting has a shining brightness, mystery, and balance • indicates the painting shows God's hand • indicates the painting shows that the sky stays beautiful even during sad times on Earth	• describes a child's impressions of the nighttime sky • indicates that the glory of the nighttime sky stays with the child even after he stops looking at it

Name _____   Date _____

Use What You Know

Think about what the sky looks like at night. List three words to describe it.

1. _____

2. _____

3. _____

Text Structure: Poem

Poets sometimes use old-fashioned words not usually found in today's English. For example, they may use *'tis* instead of *it is* or spell an *-ed* ending as *'d* (*lov'd* instead of *loved*). Underline three examples of this kind of language in the poem. Did you find this kind of language effective? Why or why not?

MARK THE TEXT

_____

_____

_____

Reading Strategy: Compare and Contrast

Find a picture of van Gogh's painting *The Starry Night* on page 194 of your textbook, in a library book, or on the Internet. Compare the painting to the poem. Circle three details in the poem that you think appear in the painting. What two things does the poem contrast in the second stanza?

MARK THE TEXT

_____

What two things does it contrast in the last two lines?

_____

_____

The sky is crack'd with radiance and seems,
To speak in tones too cosmic and too low,
For us to hear, and yet the canvas teems
With messages we guess but never know.

It speaks of balance 'tween the sky and land,
The one ablaze, the other soft and dim,
And hints the presence of a master hand,
Protecting those who sleep and trust in Him.

The stars are soft, as if they're viewed through tears,
Melting into a solemn, saddened glow,
A testament to hard and troubled years,
Yet overall the starlight serves to show,

     Amid the darkest trials of this world,
     Is beauty found in galaxies bright-swirl'd.

_____

crack'd, cracked
radiance, brightness
canvas teems with, the painting is full of
'tween, between
ablaze, on fire
solemn, very serious or sad
testament, proof
trials, difficulties or hardships

Escape at Bedtime

Robert Louis Stevenson

The lights from the parlour and kitchen shone out
Through the blinds and the windows and bars;
And high overhead and all moving about,
There were thousands of millions of stars.
There ne'er were such thousands of leaves on a tree,
Nor of people in church or the Park,
As the crowds of the stars that looked down upon me,
And that glittered and winked in the dark.
The Dog, and the Plough, and the Hunter, and all,
And the star of the sailor, and Mars,
These shown in the sky, and the pail by the wall
Would be half full of water and stars.
They saw me at last, and they chased me with cries,
And they soon had me packed into bed;
But the glory kept shining and bright in my eyes,
And the stars going round in my head.

---

parlour, living room
blinds, objects that cover windows
ne'er, never
glittered, were very shiny
Plough, a constellation resembling a farmer's tool
sailor, a person who works on a ship

Text Structure: Poem

Circle the rhymed pairs of words at the ends of lines in this poem, and draw lines connecting each rhymed pair.

MARK THE TEXT

Reading Strategy: Compare and Contrast

Compare and contrast this poem to "On van Gogh's *Starry Night*." What is similar and different about the subject of each poem?

_____

_____

_____

_____

_____

Literary Element: Personification

Personification gives human traits or abilities to things that are not human. Underline an example of personification in the poem. What is personified? What human trait or ability is given to it or them?

MARK THE TEXT

_____

_____

_____

_____

Comprehension Check

Underline the names of three constellations, or star clusters, that the speaker sees in the sky.

MARK THE TEXT

Choose one and complete:

1. Paint or draw a picture of the painting described in the first poem or the sky described in the second.

2. Write your own poem about the nighttime sky and how it makes you feel. Or, if you prefer, write a song about it.

3. Many people believe that van Gogh's *The Starry Night* shows the stars in the constellation Aries. Study van Gogh's *The Starry Night* in your textbook, in an art book, or at an Internet website. Then, in an astronomy book or website on the Internet, find a photo or drawing of the constellation Aries. Compare the two in a report.

4. Do library or Internet research to find out more about some of the stars or constellations mentioned in "Escape at Bedtime." Include your findings in a short written report.

5. How far away are the stars? Why do they twinkle? What are the names of some famous stars? Choose one of these questions, or another interesting question about the stars. Then do Internet or library research to answer the question. Present your findings in a short written or oral report.

Retell It!

Imagine that you just saw van Gogh's painting *The Starry Night* or that you are the speaker in "Escape at Bedtime." Write a diary entry about your experiences. Include details from the poem.

_____

_____

_____

_____

_____

_____

_____

Reader's Response

How did these poems and the van Gogh painting make you feel about the nighttime sky?

_____

_____

_____

_____

Think About the Skill

How did comparing and contrasting the first poem with the van Gogh painting that inspired it help you better understand or appreciate the poem, the painting, or both?

_____

_____

_____

_____

_____

_____

GRAMMAR

Use with textbook page 198.

Comparative and Superlative Adjectives
Use **comparative adjectives** to compare two people, places, or things. Use **superlative adjectives** to compare three or more people, places, or things.

Form the comparative and superlative of most one-syllable and some two-syllable adjectives like this:

Adjective	**Comparative**	**Superlative**
tall	tall**er than**	**the** tall**est**
hot	hot**ter than**	**the** hot**test**
easy	eas**ier than**	**the** eas**iest**

Use *more* and *most* to form the comparative and superlative of most adjectives with two or more syllables.

Adjective	**Comparative**	**Superlative**
helpful	**more** helpful **than**	**the most** helpful

Sometimes adjectives are irregular in the comparative and superlative forms.

Adjective	**Comparative**	**Superlative**
good	better	best
bad	worse	the worst

Read each sentence. Circle the correct form of the comparative or superlative adjective.

1. Mercury is the (most close / closest) planet to the sun.

2. Pluto is (smaller / smallest) than Earth.

3. In the solar system, Mars is (more famous / most famous) than Neptune.

4. Venus is the (hotter / hottest) planet of all.

5. That is the (brighter / brightest) star in the sky.

GRAMMAR

Use after the lesson on comparative and superlative adverbs.

Comparative and Superlative Adverbs

An adverb is a word that describes a verb, an adjective, or another adverb. Adverbs answer the questions *Where? When? In what manner?* and *To what extent?* Use **comparative adverbs** to compare two things. Use **superlative adverbs** to compare three or more things.

Here is how to form the comparative and superlative with *-ly* words.

adverb	comparative adverb	superlative adverb
quickly	**more** quickly **than**	**the most** quickly

Here is how to form the comparative and superlative with one-syllable adverbs.

fast	fast**er than**	the fast**est**

Some adverbs are irregular.

well	**better**	**the best**
badly	**worse**	**the worst**

Complete these sentences. Use the comparative or superlative form of the adverbs (in parentheses).

Example: Some comets glow (brightly) _____*more brightly*_____ than others.

1. The moon is shining (brilliantly)_____ tonight than last night.

2. Sunspots appear (clearly) _____ in photographs than in movies.

3. What moves the (rapidly) _____ of all the objects in the sky?

4. I think Vincent van Gogh can paint (well) _____ than anyone else.

5. Does gravity on Earth pull (hard) _____ than on Mars?

Name _____ Date _____

SKILLS FOR WRITING

Use with textbook page 199.

Using the Internet to Do Research Reports

The purpose of a research report is to give factual information about a topic. The Internet can be a valuable tool as you look for facts about a subject. Not all information on the Internet is accurate. Be sure your facts are correct by checking several sources.

Read the sample Internet search results below. Answer the questions that follow.

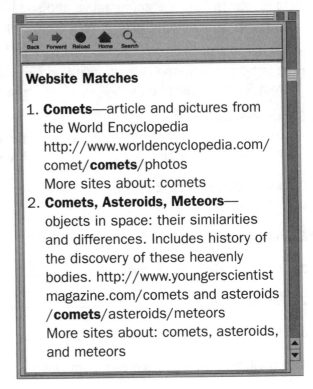

▲ Screen 1   ▲ Screen 2

1. Look at Screen 1. What is the subject of this Internet search? _____

2. Look at Screen 2: Which site contains information for younger readers?

   _____

3. Look at Screen 2: Which site explains the difference between comets and asteroids?

   _____

4. Look at Screen 2: In which site are there pictures of comets?

   _____

5. Where would you look to find more information about asteroids?

   _____

PROOFREADING AND EDITING

Use with textbook page 200.

Read the research report about Vincent van Gogh carefully. Find all the mistakes. Remember to check for mistakes in the use of comparative and superlative adjectives. Then rewrite the report correctly on the lines below.

Vincent van Gogh

Vincent van Gogh is one of the world's most great artists. He painted landscapes and peoples? Van Gogh created some very well-known paintings *The Starry Night* is famouser than his works. Many people think it is his better piece. in this painting the painted stars are yellower than real stars in the sky. Sadly, van Gogh was one of the unluckyer artists to ever live. During his lifetime, he only sold one panting. Today, his paintings are worth millions of dollars.

_____

_____

_____

_____

_____

_____

_____

_____

_____

_____

_____

_____

_____

Name _____ Date _____

SPELLING

Use after the spelling lesson.

Changing *y* to *i* Before Adding -*er*, -*est*

To form a comparative of adjectives that end in *y*, change the **y** to **i** and add **-er**.

    scary   scari + **er**   scar**ier**   easy   easi + **er**   eas**ier**

To form the superlative of adjectives that ends in *y*, change the **y** to **i** and add **-est**.

    scary   scari + **est**   scar**iest**   easy   easi + **est**   eas**iest**

Write the comparative and superlative form of each word.

Example: friendly   *friendlier*   *friendliest*

1. tiny _____ _____

2. icy _____ _____

3. rocky _____ _____

4. starry _____ _____

5. shiny _____ _____

6. heavy _____ _____

7. early _____ _____

8. easy _____ _____

9. chunky _____ _____

10. sunny _____ _____

UNIT 5 Reach for the Stars
PART 2

Contents

VOCABULARY

Use with textbook page 203.

Read each sentence. Circle the letter of the word that defines the underlined word.

1. The mortals knew that they would not live forever.

    a. people   b. gods   c. animals   d. plants

2. I feel content when I have no problems.

    a. bothered   b. unhappy   c. happy   d. worried

3. The disobedient child did not mind her parents.

    a. badly behaved   b. well-behaved   c. polite   d. pleasant

4. We gave our beloved teacher a bouquet of flowers to show our thanks.

    a. disliked   b. adored   c. unkind   d. new

5. The toothache caused him unbearable pain.

    a. agreeable   b. satisfying   c. enjoyable   d. terrible

Read the clues. Use the words in the box to complete the crossword puzzle. (Hint: You will not use all of the words.)

unbearable	beloved	condemned	disobedient
appearance	content	portrayed	destruction

ACROSS

3. not doing as you are told

4. adored, much liked

5. happy or satisfied

DOWN

1. having a quality you cannot stand

2. sentenced; judged against

VOCABULARY BUILDING

Understanding Greek and Latin Roots

Many English words have **roots**, or word parts, that come from the ancient Greek and Latin languages. Look at the underlined word in each sentence. Each word contains the Greek root *astro* (*aster*). This root means "star."

The **astro**nomer studied the stars.   An **aster** is a star-shaped flower.
An **aster**isk (*) is a star-shaped mark.

Knowing the meaning of Latin and Greek roots can help you to figure out the meanings of unfamiliar words.

Study the charts below with Greek and Latin roots.

Greek Roots	
Root	**Meaning**
cosmo	universe
tele	far away
graph	write
therm	heat
chron	time

Latin Roots	
Root	**Meaning**
cogn	know
mob	move
ject	throw
port	carry
duct	lead

Use the roots in the chart to help you choose the meaning of each word listed below. Write the letter for the correct meaning of each word. Hint: Look at the underlined words in the definitions.

_____ **1.** microcosm

_____ **2.** portable

_____ **3.** telescope

_____ **4.** biography

_____ **5.** thermometer

_____ **6.** chronological

_____ **7.** eject

_____ **8.** conductor

_____ **9.** recognize

_____ **10.** mobile

a. <u>throw</u> out

b. instrument that enlarges images of <u>faraway</u> stars

c. able of <u>moving</u>

d. to see someone and <u>know</u> who the person is

e. instrument that measures <u>heat</u>

f. one who <u>leads</u> a band or orchestra

g. a little world, or <u>universe</u>

h. arranged in <u>time</u> order

i. can be <u>carried</u>

j. <u>written</u> story of a person's life

READING STRATEGY

Use with textbook page 203.

Identifying Causes and Effects
Identifying causes and effects can help you better understand a text. Some texts tell about events that happen and why these events happen. *Why* an event happens is the **cause**. *What happens* as a result of a cause is the **effect**. Look for the words *so* and *because*, since they are often signals of causes and effects.

        cause   **effect**
The moon hid the entire sun, **so** there was a total eclipse.

           cause   **effect**
Because the night sky was beautiful, the artist painted a picture of it.

Read the following sentences. Draw one line under the cause. Draw two lines under the effect. Circle the signal word.

1. Sunspots look darker than other parts of the sun because cooler gases give off less light than hotter gases.

2. Because meteorites crashed onto the moon's surface, it was covered with holes and craters.

3. Astronauts could not survive on the planet Venus because the planet's temperature is too hot.

4. Last night was too cloudy, so we couldn't see any stars in the sky.

5. I was interested in astronomy so I wrote my research report on the zodiac constellations.

Use with textbook pages 212–214.

Summary: Solar Eclipses

A solar eclipse happens when the moon moves directly between Earth and the sun. The moon makes a shadow on the surface of Earth. From Earth, it looks as though the moon has blocked out the sun's light. This article tells how to make a special viewing box that lets you watch an eclipse safely.

Visual Summary

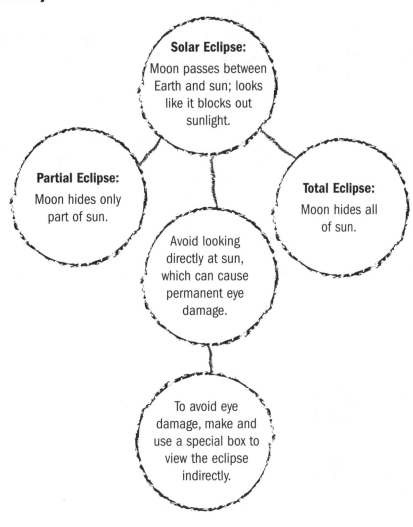

Solar Eclipse:
Moon passes between Earth and sun; looks like it blocks out sunlight.

Partial Eclipse:
Moon hides only part of sun.

Total Eclipse:
Moon hides all of sun.

Avoid looking directly at sun, which can cause permanent eye damage.

To avoid eye damage, make and use a special box to view the eclipse indirectly.

Solar Eclipses

A solar eclipse occurs when the moon passes directly between Earth and the sun, casting a shadow on the surface of the Earth. From Earth, it looks as if the moon has blocked out the light of the sun.

Eclipses may be partial or total. A partial eclipse occurs when the moon hides only part of the sun. A total eclipse occurs when the sun is completely hidden by the moon. Total eclipses of the sun are very rare, occurring about once every three hundred sixty years in the same location. However, several solar eclipses may occur each year.

In ancient times, people were frightened by solar eclipses because they did not know what was happening. Now eclipses are of great interest to astronomers and to the public. Eclipses provide an opportunity to view the sun's outer atmosphere, the solar corona.

_____

rare, unusual; not common

Use What You Know

Write what you know about the relationship or position of the Earth, the sun, and the moon.

_____

_____

_____

Text Structure: Science Article

A science article presents information on a topic in science. Often it explains or defines key terms. Circle the key term explained in the **MARK THE TEXT** first paragraph and underline the words that explain it. What is the difference between a partial and total solar eclipse?

_____

_____

_____

_____

Reading Strategy: Identifying Causes and Effects

Underline people's reaction to solar eclipses in ancient **MARK THE TEXT** times. What caused them to react this way?

_____

_____

Choose one and complete:
1. Draw pictures showing the steps to take when viewing a solar eclipse.
2. Imagine that you are filming a solar eclipse for a TV documentary. What music would you use in the background? Describe the music, or make an audiocassette or CD of it.
3. Do library or Internet research to find out more about solar eclipses in history. Present your findings on a timeline or in another written form.

Never look directly at the sun. It can cause **permanent** eye damage or **blindness**. If you have the chance to view a solar eclipse, you can make an eclipse-viewing box to view it safely.

Eclipse-Viewing Box

You will need:
- a long box or tube
- a pair of scissors
- a piece of aluminum foil
- tape
- a pin
- a sheet of white paper

1. Find or make a long box or tube. The length of the box is important. The longer the box, the bigger the image you will see.
2. Carefully cut a hole in the center of one end of the box.
3. Tape the piece of foil over the hole.

---

permanent, lasting for all time
blindness, the condition of being unable to see

Reading Strategy: Identifying Causes and Effects

Underline what you should never do according to the first paragraph on this page. What can it cause?

MARK THE TEXT

_____

_____

Text Structure: Science Article

Science articles often include experiments that list the items you will need to perform the experiment and then give a numbered list of steps in the experiment. Circle the items needed for this experiment. For which step on this page would you use scissors?

MARK THE TEXT

_____

_____

Reading Strategy: Identifying Causes and Effects

Underline what step 1 says is important. What will it result in?

MARK THE TEXT

_____

_____

Reading Strategy:
Identifying Causes and Effects

Underline where you should put the sheet of white paper. What effect does the paper have?

MARK THE TEXT

_____

_____

Comprehension Check

Circle the main thing to do in the last paragraph. When do you need to move the box so that the sides don't cast a shadow?

MARK THE TEXT

_____

_____

_____

Text Structure: Science Article

Science articles often include warnings to help people avoid danger when doing experiments. Circle the warning repeated at the end. Based on what you read earlier in the article, why is it dangerous to ignore this warning?

MARK THE TEXT

_____

_____

4. Make a small hole in the aluminum foil with the pin. This hole is what the light from the eclipse will go through.
5. Cut a viewing hole in the side of the box. This is where you will see the **image** of the solar eclipse.
6. Tape the sheet of paper inside the end of the box near the viewing **portal**. The paper should be flat against the end that is opposite the pinhole.

   Point the end of the box with the pinhole at the sun so that you see a round image on the paper at the other end. If you are having trouble pointing the box at the eclipse, look at the shadow of the box on the ground. Move the box so that the shadow looks like the end of the box (so the sides of the box are not casting a shadow). The round spot of light you see on the paper is a pinhole image of the sun. *Remember: Do not look at the sun! Look only at the image on the paper.*

_____

image, a picture of
   something
portal, hole for viewing

Retell It!

On a separate sheet of paper, draw pictures that show each step in making the eclipse-viewing box. Label your drawings. Then, on the lines below, tell others how to make the box, using your pictures.

_____

_____

_____

_____

_____

_____

_____

_____

_____

_____

Reader's Response

What did you find most interesting in this article? Why?

_____

_____

_____

_____

Think About the Skill

How did identifying causes and effects help you better understand the article?

_____

_____

_____

_____

GRAMMAR

Use with textbook page 216.

The Passive Voice

A sentence can be in **active voice** or **passive voice**.

Active: We made the telescope.
Passive: The telescope was made by us.

Read each sentence. In the space provided, write *active* or *passive*.

1. I used a special viewer for looking at eclipses. _____

2. The viewer was made by my friend Manuel. _____

3. We looked at the sun through the viewer. _____

4. The sunlight was blocked by the moon. _____

5. The sky was darkened by the eclipse. _____

6. The bright noonday sun hurt our eyes. _____

Rewrite the sentences using the passive voice.

7. The hot rays scorched the crops.

_____

_____

8. The hot sun even burned the skin of the Huichols.

_____

_____

Rewrite the sentences using the active voice.

9. The sun was named by the boy.

_____

_____

10. The Earth was no longer threatened by the sun.

_____

_____

GRAMMAR

Use after the lesson on compound and complex sentences.

A **compound sentence** usually has two or more independent clauses joined with a comma and a coordinating conjunction such as *for, and, nor, but, yet* or *so.*

A **complex sentence** has one independent clause and at least one dependent clause. The clauses are joined by a subordinating conjunction such as *so that, if, since* or *because.*

Read each sentence from the selections. Write *compound* or *complex* in the space provided. Underline the independent clause or clauses in each sentence. Circle the coordinating or subordinating conjunction.

_____ 1. The ten suns became tired of this routine, so they all decided to appear at the same time.

_____ 2. One day Re wept, and humans were created from his tears.

_____ 3. The Hiuchol people loved and respected the sun, for a god lived within it.

_____ 4. Because the sun was so close, Earth became hotter and hotter.

_____ 5. The people wanted Tou to go higher into the sky, but Tou could not bear to live far from the Earth.

_____ 6. "I'll go with you, Tou, if you will travel higher in the sky."

_____ 7. Again the people told him to go even higher, for it was still too hot.

_____ 8. Three more times Tou stopped, and each time the people told him to go higher.

_____ 9. The boy was there too, so the sun didn't feel lonely.

_____ 10. The people were content, too, for Earth was no longer burning hot.

SKILLS FOR WRITING

Use with textbook page 217.

Quoting and Paraphrasing

A **quotation** is a restatement of a person's exact words. When you use a quotation in a report, place quotation marks (" ") before and after the words. Use the exact punctuation, capitalization, and spelling of the original text.

Dr. Cosmos writes, "Total eclipses are very rare."

A **paraphrase** is the restatement of someone else's words—in your own words. Do not use quotation marks when you paraphrase. You can often use the word *that* to introduce an idea you are paraphrasing.

Dr. Stargazer writes that total eclipses don't occur very often.

Put the correct punctuation around each quotation.

1. Dr. Patel writes, Staring into an eclipse can be very dangerous. You must protect your eyes at all costs!

2. The journalist reports, More than 15,000 people waited to see the rare eclipse of the sun.

3. Dr. Pam Gabor writes, The Huichol myth tells how a small boy saved his people from the sun's hot rays.

Paraphrase each quotation.

4. The newspaper reports, "Today, children and adults all over the world read and enjoy ancient myths."

_____

_____

_____

5. Jack Garcia writes, "The ancient sun god Re was often pictured with the head of a falcon."

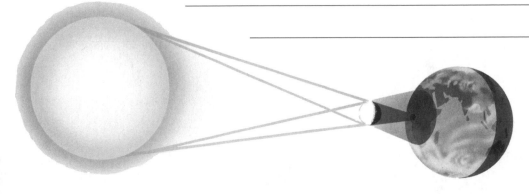

_____

_____

PROOFREADING AND EDITING

Use with textbook page 218.

Read the report below carefully. Find all the mistakes. Be sure to look for mistakes with the passive and active voices and with the use of quotation marks. Then rewrite the report correctly on the lines below.

The egyptian Sun God

The son god Re, sometimes called "ra," was an ancient Egyptian god. Professor Diane johnson reports, Of all the Egyptian gods, Re was most important to the Egyptians.

egyptians, believed that re was the creator of all things. He was also very active on the world she created. During the daytime Re traveled by boat and brought the sun across the sky. During the Evening Re fought with terrible monsters? Professor Johnson writes, Re was quite a guy! He known by three names. These names related to the position of the Sun at dawn, at noon, and at dusk

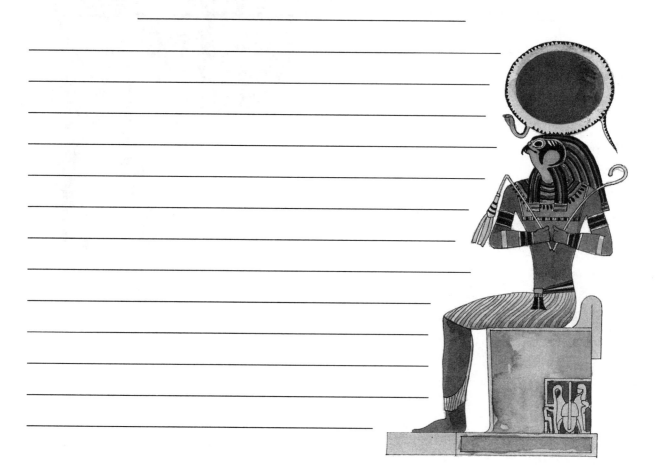

_____

_____

_____

_____

_____

_____

_____

_____

_____

_____

_____

_____

_____

SPELLING

Use after the spelling lesson.

Double the Final Consonant and Add -ed

Some words change their spelling when -ed is added to them.

In a one-syllable word that ends with a short vowel + single consonant, double the final consonant before adding -ed.

plan + ed	planned	stir + ed	stirred
drum + ed	drummed	skid + ed	skidded

Add -ed to each word below.

Example: sled _____*sledded*_____

1. drip _____

2. star _____

3. rip _____

4. trot _____

5. fan _____

6. drop _____

7. clip _____

8. stop _____

9. scrub _____

10. pin _____

UNIT 6 Shifting Perspectives

Contents

VOCABULARY

Use with textbook page 229.

Read the words in the box. Choose one to complete each sentence and write it on the line. You will use each word once.

| absorbed | range | transmitted | surface | double |

1. The message was _____ over the radio so that everyone got the news.

2. Two babies can ride at the same time in a _____ stroller.

3. The lecture covered a wide _____ of topics from art to mathematics.

4. The _____ of the table was polished and shined.

5. The sponge quickly _____ the water that had spilled.

Read the clues. Use the words in the box to complete the crossword puzzle. (Hint: You will not use all the words.)

| radio | opaque | plane | convex | reflected | X rays | gamma |

ACROSS

3. This means "bounced off."

4. This kind of mirror is curved outward.

DOWN

1. These waves carry information through television.

2. This kind of mirror is flat.

5. These electromagnetic waves are used to photograph bones.

VOCABULARY BUILDING

Understanding Number Words, Including Ordinals

Use **number words** when you want to tell how many of something; for example: *My sister has* **two** *radios*. Use **ordinals** when you want to tell where something is in a series of things; for example: *Hector was the* **second** *person in line*. Look at the examples below.

Number Words		Ordinals	
1	one	1st	first
2	two	2nd	second
3	three	3rd	third
4	four	4th	fourth
5	five	5th	fifth
10	ten	10th	tenth
25	twenty-five	25th	twenty-fifth
50	fifty	50th	fiftieth
100	one hundred	100th	one hundredth
1,000	one thousand	1,000th	one thousandth

Complete the sentences using number words or ordinals from the chart.

1. I arrived earlier than everybody else, so I bought my ticket _____.

2. They have been married for ten years, so today is their _____ anniversary.

3. If there are four people in line, the last person is _____ in line.

4. The lead runner came in _____ because somebody pulled ahead of her at the last minute.

5. Today is his fiftieth birthday, so he is _____ years old.

Write a sentence for each of the words below.

6. third _____

7. ten _____

8. twenty-fifth _____

9. hundred _____

10. thousand _____

READING STRATEGY

Use with textbook page 229.

Monitoring Comprehension

To make sure that you understand what you are reading, try **monitoring your comprehension**. Follow these five steps:

- Reread the part you don't understand.
- See if you can restate, or paraphrase, the text using your own words.
- Make a list of words you don't understand. Use context clues or a dictionary to figure out what they mean.
- Make up a list of questions about things that you found confusing.
- Look in the text for answers to your questions. If you can't find them, ask your teacher for help.

Read the first page of "Light" on page 230 in your textbook. Then, use each of the five steps listed above to monitor your comprehension.

1. Pause and think about what you read. Now, try reading it again. Pay special attention to words or ideas you didn't understand the first time. What are these two paragraphs about?

_____

_____

2. Paraphrase the first two sentences. Restate them using your own words.

_____

_____

3. List two words you found difficult to understand and write down their definitions. Use a dictionary if necessary.

_____

_____

4. Write down a question you have about what you read.

_____

_____

5. Use your text to answer the question. If you can't find the answer, or can't understand what you find, ask your teacher for help.

_____

_____

Use with textbook pages 240–242.

Summary: Mirror, Mirror: Mambo No. 5

This passage is about a restaurant in Miami, Florida, a city where many people from Cuba now live. The restaurant is called the Versailles. Mirrors cover the walls and ceiling of this restaurant, and people there can see multiple reflections of themselves and others. The author likes to think that the restaurant's mirrors have a memory, absorbing the history of the many Cubans who have lived and died in Miami.

Visual Summary

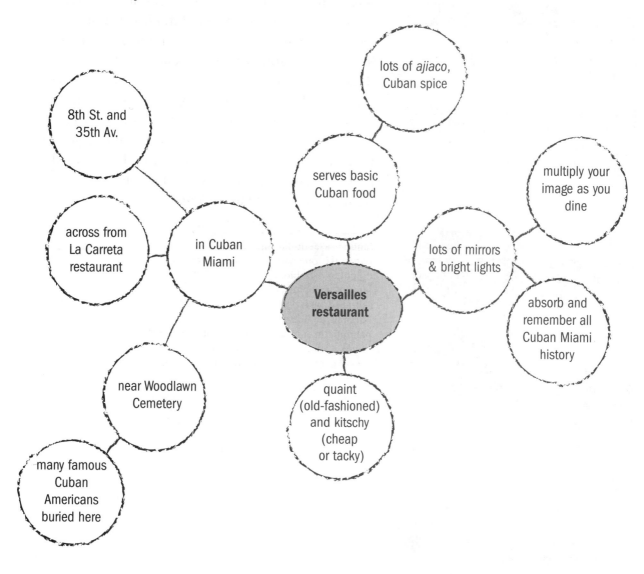

Mirror, Mirror: Mambo No. 5

Gustavo Pérez Firmat

One of the landmarks of Cuban Miami is a restaurant called Versailles, which has been located on Eighth Street and Thirty-fifth Avenue for many years. About the only thing this Versailles shares with its French namesake is that it has lots of mirrors on its walls. One goes to the Versailles not only to be seen, but to be multiplied. This quaint, kitschy, noisy restaurant that serves basic Cuban food is a paradise for the self-absorbed: the Nirvana of Little Havana. Because of the bright lights, even the windows reflect. The Versailles is a Cuban panopticon: you can lunch, but you can't hide. Who goes there wants to make a spectacle of himself (or herself). All the *ajiaco* you can eat and all the jewelry you can wear multiplied by the number of reflecting planes—and to top it off, a waitress who calls you *mi vida*.

---

landmarks, familiar sights
namesake, one having the same name as another
quaint, old-fashioned
kitschy, cheap or tacky
self-absorbed, people who like themselves very much
Nirvana, paradise
panopticon, a place where everyone can be observed
ajiaco, a spice used in Cuban cooking
mi vida, my life (term of endearment in Spanish)

Name _____ Date _____

Across the street at La Carreta, another popular restaurant, the food is the same (both establishments are owned by the same man) but the feel is different. Instead of mirrors La Carreta has booths. There you can ensconce yourself in a booth and not be faced with multiple images of yourself. But at the Versailles there is no choice but to bask in self-reflective glory.

For years I have harbored the fantasy that those mirrors retain the blurred image of everyone who has paraded before them. I think the mirrors have a memory, as when one turns off the TV and the shadowy figures remain on the screen. Every Cuban who has lived or set foot in Miami over the last three decades has, at one time or another, seen himself or herself reflected on those shiny surfaces. It's no coincidence that the Versailles sits only two blocks away from the Woodlawn Cemetery, which contains the remains of many Cuban notables, including Desi Arnaz's father, whose remains occupy a niche right above Gerardo Machado's. Has anybody ever counted the number of Cubans who have died in Miami? Miami is a Cuban city not only because of the number of Cubans who live there but also because of the number who have died there.

---

ensconce yourself, install yourself
bask in self-reflective glory, enjoy your own reflection
harbored the fantasy, had the idea
retain, keep

Comprehension Check

Underline the detail about the seats in La Carreta. How is **MARK THE TEXT** dining there different from dining at Versailles?

_____

_____

_____

Reading Strategy: Recognizing Fantasy

Fantasy is highly imaginative writing that could not happen in the real world. Circle the writer's ideas about the mirrors that are **MARK THE TEXT** fantasy. What do the mirrors seem to represent for him?

_____

_____

_____

Text Structure: Essay

An essay often contains the thoughts and feelings of the person writing it. Underline the writer's thoughts about why Miami is a Cuban city. What do you think he means? **MARK THE TEXT**

_____

_____

_____

_____

_____

Comprehension Check

Underline what the writer calls Versailles in the first sentence **MARK THE TEXT** and the kind of house he calls it later. What is he saying about Versailles?

_____

_____

_____

Reading Strategy: Recognizing Fantasy

Circle the writer's fantasy about the time when he has to pay for his **MARK THE TEXT** last *ajiaco*. What time does he mean?

_____

_____

Text Structure: Essay

Underline what the writer says his idea of immortality is. **MARK THE TEXT** What do his thoughts show about the importance he places on his heritage as a Cuban American?

_____

_____

_____

_____

The Versailles is a glistening mausoleum. The history of Little Havana—tragic , comic, tragicomic—is written on those spectacular walls. This may have been why, when the mirrors came down in 1991, there was such an uproar that some of them had to be put back. The hall of mirrors is also a house of spirits. When the time comes for me to pay for my last *ajiaco*, I intend to disappear into one of the mirrors (I would prefer the one on the right, just above the espresso machine). My idea of immortality is to become a mirror image at the Versailles.

_____

glistening, shiny
mausoleum, a place where dead people are buried
tragic, very sad
comic, funny
uproar, a lot of noise or angry protest against something
intend, plan
immortality, living forever

Choose one and complete:
1. Imagine you are making a movie that is set in Cuban Miami. Draw the setting for a scene in this restaurant, or create a small model of it.
2. Do library or Internet research to learn more about the French Versailles, Little Havana, Desi Arnaz, and Gerardo Machado. Then write four footnotes to explain these details.
3. Using the Internet, find out more about food and beverages served in Cuban or other Latin American restaurants. Then create a possible menu for the restaurant described in this essay.

Retell It!

Describe the Versailles restaurant from the viewpoint of a waitress, the owner, or someone else who is there every day.

_____

_____

_____

_____

_____

Reader's Response

What memories or feelings about your own cultural heritage did the essay remind you of?

_____

_____

_____

_____

_____

Think About the Skill

How did recognizing fantasy help you better understand the essay?

_____

_____

_____

_____

_____

GRAMMAR

Use with textbook page 244.

Subject and Object Pronouns

- A **subject pronoun** replaces a noun that is the subject of a sentence.
  Tommy went to the museum.   **He** really enjoyed looking at art.

- An **object pronoun** replaces a noun that is an object (after the verb).
  Rachel bought a **mirror**.   Rachel put **it** in her bedroom.

	Subject Pronouns	Object Pronouns
Singular	I, you, he, she, it	me, you, him, her, it
Plural	we, you, they	us, you, them

Read the sentence pairs below. Circle each pronoun in the second sentence. Underline the noun it refers to, or replaces, in the first sentence.

Example: The underline{museum} is open on Sunday. (It) is closed on Monday.

1. Kim wanted to go to the museum. She liked looking at paintings.

2. Kim needed tickets. Kim bought them in advance.

3. Kim invited Matt. Kim gave him a ticket.

4. Kim and Matt went to lunch first. They ate hamburgers.

5. Kim and Matt saw a beautiful painting. Kim and Matt liked it a lot.

6. The gift shop sells books and cards. It also sells jewelry.

7. Matt went to the gift shop. He bought a postcard.

8. Kim waited for Matt for a long time. Then Kim saw him.

9. Kim looked at the postcard. She wanted to buy a card, too.

10. The museum was closing. It closed at 6:00 P.M.

GRAMMAR

Use after the lesson on nominative and objective cases.

Nominative and Objective Cases

Case is the form a noun or pronoun takes, depending on how it is used in a sentence.
A noun or pronoun used as the subject of a sentence is in the **nominative case.**

    Dad loves Cuban food.
    He loves Cuban food.

A noun or pronoun used as the object of a sentence is in the **objective case.**

    The waiter helped *Lucy* and *Rita*.
    The waiter helped *them*.

Look at each underlined word. Write down the name of its case.

Example: The <u>restaurant</u> is in Little Havana. _____*nominative*_____

1. <u>We</u> ate dinner at Andy's favorite restaurant. _____

2. The mirrors reflect <u>images</u> of people eating. _____

3. <u>Ana</u> sat next to me. _____

4. The waiter saw <u>her</u>. _____

5. <u>They</u> are neighbors. _____

Complete each sentence with a noun or pronoun. Use the case in parentheses ( ).

6. (nominative) _____ enjoyed the meal very much.

7. (nominative) _____ opened a new restaurant.

8. The menu includes (objective) _____.

9. All of the customers enjoy (objective) _____.

10. (nominative) _____ is a great success.

SKILLS FOR WRITING

Use with textbook page 245.

Writing Responses

A **response** states your personal reaction to something you have read or seen. It should include your feelings and thoughts. One way to organize a response is to begin with general information. Then you can give details that tell more specific information.

The essay "Mirror, Mirror: Mambo No. 5" on pages 240–242 in your textbook is a personal response to a restaurant in Miami, where the author grew up. Read the essay again and think about your own response to the essay. Then answer the questions below.

1. What is one piece of general information from the text?

_____

2. What is one piece of specific information from the text?

_____

3. How does this essay make you feel? Why?

_____

_____

4. Would you like to visit Versailles restaurant based on what you've read? Why?

_____

_____

5. Did you like or dislike his essay? Why?

_____

_____

6-10. Now use your answers to the questions above to write a five-sentence response to "Mirror, Mirror: Mambo No. 5" in the space provided below.

_____

_____

_____

_____

_____

_____

PROOFREADING AND EDITING

Use with textbook page 246.

Read the essay carefully. Find and circle all the mistakes. Be sure to look for mistakes in the use of subject and object pronouns. Rewrite the essay correctly on the lines below.

<u>Liberation</u> by M. C. Escher

M. C. escher's painting Liberation is an exciting work of art. They is a picture of triangles that change into bird shapes The change happens as your eye travels upward. When your eye reaches the top of the canvas. the birds scatter into the sky. At first glance, I saw only birds. It seemed to fill the painting. Me didn't even notice the triangles at the bottom. My friend Herman had to point them out to I. He showed me where the triangles begin at the bottom of the painting. Then he pointed how them change into bird shapes, a little bit at a time. First, the straight edges become wavy. Then, the head, tails, and wings forms. Finally, the triangles have become bird of all different shapes.

_____

_____

_____

_____

_____

_____

_____

_____

_____

_____

_____

SPELLING

Use after the spelling lesson.

Adding -ed

Add **-ed** to regular verbs to form the **past tense**. Follow these spelling rules:

- If the verb ends with a consonant and *e*, just add *-d*.
  bake   bake + *d* = baked   provide   provide + *d* = provided

- If a one-syllable verb ends with a short vowel + single consonant, double the final consonant before adding *-ed*.
  skip   skipp + *ed* = skipped   pat   patt + *ed* = patted

- If the verb ends with two consonants, or has a vowel combination, just add *-ed*.
  fill   fill + *ed* = filled   treat   treat + *ed* = treated

Form the past tense of the following verbs by adding *-ed*.

1. call _____

2. reflect _____

3. trade _____

4. trap _____

5. paint _____

Complete each sentence using the verb in parentheses ( ) in the past tense.

6. I (drop) _____ the mirror, but it did not break.

7. The light (bounce) _____ off of the mirror.

8. Suddenly, a bright light (fill) _____ the room.

9. The strong light (create) _____ interesting images.

10. I (turn) _____ off the light.

UNIT 6 Shifting Perspectives
PART 2

Contents

VOCABULARY

Use with textbook page 249.

Read the words in the box. Choose a word from the box to complete each sentence. You will use each word once.

| sorrow | imitate | barrier | tangible | defects |

1. One way in which children learn is to watch adults and _____ their actions.

2. Sheila cried and felt great _____ when she heard the sad news.

3. I don't like gifts that I can't touch as much as I like _____ things.

4. James inspected his new suit to make sure it had no _____.

5. There was a _____ blocking the path and a sign that said, "Do Not Enter."

Read the clues. Use the words in the box to complete the crossword puzzle. (Hint: You will not use all the words.)

| barrier | repentance | quiet | illness | tangible | imitate | defect | sorrow |

ACROSS
4. feeling bad about, or regret for doing something wrong
5. sadness

DOWN
1. flaw or mistake
2. something blocking your path
3. sickness

VOCABULARY BUILDING

Using Print and Online Resources to Find Spellings, Meanings, and Related Words

- **Using a Dictionary**

Start with the first few letters of the word you want to spell. For example, if you don't know whether it's spelled *sorrow, sorow,* or *sorro*, scan the entries that begin with *sor-*. You should be able to find the word and its definition. Many words have more than one meaning. The first meaning given is the most common meaning of the word. See if the meaning makes sense in the context of your sentence. If it doesn't, keep reading the other definitions.

- **Using a Thesaurus**

The main reason for using a thesaurus is to find synonyms, but it can be useful for other purposes, too. If you have no idea how to spell a word, look up the entry for a synonym that you do know how to spell. For example, *sorrow* would be listed in the entry for *sadness* as a synonym or a related word. If you look up a word in the dictionary and don't understand the definition, sometimes knowing its synonyms will help you. Use a thesaurus to see other words with similar meanings.

- **Using an Online Dictionary and Thesaurus**

To check a word's spelling in an online dictionary, write down the ways you think the word might be spelled. Then, enter these words into the search box, one at a time. Only the correct spelling will return the definition of the word. If you can't find your word using an online dictionary, try an online thesaurus. As with a print thesaurus, look up an entry for a synonym. The word you're looking for should appear as a synonym or a related word.

1. Look up *languor* in an online or print dictionary.

   Write its definition. _____

2. Look up *defect* in an online or print thesaurus.

   List two synonyms. _____   _____

3. List two meanings. _____   _____

4. Look up *barrier* in an online or print thesaurus.

   Write a related word. _____

5. Look up *tangible* in an online or print thesaurus.

   What is listed as the antonym? _____

READING STRATEGY

Use with textbook page 249.

Listening to Texts

Listening to a text is similar to reading one. You can use many of the same strategies that you use when you read. Here are some tips for listening to a selection:

First: Listen without reading along. Try to create a mental image of what is being described. Don't worry about individual words. Focus instead on the main ideas or events.

Second: Read along the second time you listen to the selection. Try to connect the words you read with what you hear.

Third: Read the selection on your own. Remember your purpose for reading.

Listen to the recording of Chapter 1 of *from The Story of My Life,* which is also on page 250 in your textbook.

1. Sketch a picture of something you visualized while listening in the box below.

2. What do you think is the main idea? _____

_____

3. Write down some of the most important ideas you heard. _____

_____

_____

_____

4. After you listen a second time—while following along with the text—write a summary

of the chapter. _____

_____

_____

_____

5. What was your purpose for reading the text? _____

_____

Use with textbook pages 258–260.

Summary: "Sowing the Seeds of Peace"

This article tells about a special summer camp for teenagers from countries in the Middle East, a place of war for many years. At the camp, teenagers are encouraged to play together, talk about the conflicts between their countries, and learn from one another. The camp hopes that the teenagers' experiences will someday help bring peace to the Middle East.

Visual Summary

What?	Seeds of Peace International Camp
When?	now
Where?	Maine
Who?	teenagers from the Middle East
Why?	to confront Middle Eastern tensions and help bring groups together
How?	by having them attend summer camp together and discuss their differences

Name _____ Date _____

Sowing the Seeds of Peace

Mandy Terc

One rainy rest hour at a summer camp in Maine, fifteen-year-old Noor from the Palestinian West Bank was learning to write her name. She glanced back quickly at the example that sixteen-year-old Shirlee, a Jewish Israeli from a seaside town, had provided. After a few more seconds of intense writing, Noor triumphantly handed the piece of paper to me, her **bunk** counselor. Parading across the top of the paper in large, careful print were the Hebrew letters that spelled her Arabic name.

A spontaneous lesson on the Hebrew and Arabic alphabets probably does not happen at most summer camp bunks, but the Seeds of Peace International Camp challenges the traditional definition of what teenagers can learn and accomplish at a summer camp. Seeds of Peace brings Middle Eastern teenagers from Israel, the Palestinian National Authority, Jordan, Egypt, and other countries to Maine to help them **confront** the conflict and violence that has defined their region for more than fifty years.

At this camp, things like table and bunk assignments, sports teams and seating are never accidental. They are all part of encouraging **interaction**. Here, Israelis and Arabs not only meet for the first time but also sleep side by side, share a sink and participate in group games. In the close quarters of tiny cabins and bunk beds, bunk counselors encourage the campers to ignore national and ethnic **boundaries** as they make friends with their immediate neighbors.

---

sowing, planting
bunk, cabin
confront, deal with in a direct way
interaction, action or communication between or among people
boundaries, borders or barriers

The three weeks spent in Maine combine ordinary camp activities with a daily two-hour coexistence session, during which trained facilitators encourage discussion of political and personal issues. The remainder of the day is spent in traditional summer camp activities.

Teenagers are asked to analyze questions that have perplexed world leaders, and even bedtime can become a political forum. In my bunk, I asked the girls to summarize one positive and one negative aspect of their day before going to sleep. Sometimes, the discussions were about quite ordinary and uncontroversial things.

At other times, our bedtime discussions reflected the complexity and difficulties of living with perceived enemies. On one occasion, Adar, a strongly nationalistic Israeli, began by expressing frustration with a Palestinian girl's comment that Israel unjustly occupied Jerusalem, which the Palestinian felt truly belonged to the Palestinian people.

Instantly, eight bodies snapped from snug sleeping positions to tense, upright postures. Jerusalem is the most contentious issue between the Arab and Israeli campers, and each girl in the bunk was poised to take this opportunity to talk about her opinion on the disputed city. Adar asked if all Palestinians refused to recognize Israelis as legitimate residents of the city.

---

facilitators, people who encourage discussion about specific topics
traditional summer camp activities, sports; games
perplexed, puzzled or confused
perceived, seeming to be a certain way
contentious, likely to cause argument and disagreement
legitimate, lawful or right

Choose one and complete:
1. Draw a picture of a scene or activity at the Seeds of Peace camp.
2. List items that you would bring if you were going to the Seeds of Peace camp. Include items related to your background or family that you might want to show to others from a different background.
3. Imagine you are interviewing people at the Seeds of Peace camp for a radio show. List the questions you might ask.

Comprehension Check

Underline what the three weeks at the Maine camp combine.
MARK THE TEXT
What do you think a "coexistence session" is?

_____

_____

_____

Reading Strategy: Recognizing Cause and Effect Relationships

Circle what the writer has the girls in her bunk do at night.
MARK THE TEXT
What effect does this have on the campers?

_____

_____

_____

_____

_____

Text Structure: Social Studies Article

Underline the most contentious issue between the campers.
MARK THE TEXT
What do the campers' reactions help you understand about Middle Eastern tensions?

_____

_____

_____

Text Structure: Social Studies Article

Social studies articles often contain details about geography and culture. Underline the information about holy sites in the city of Jerusalem. **MARK THE TEXT** What do you think of the two girls' views about whom the city rightfully belongs to?

_____

_____

_____

_____

_____

Comprehension Check

Underline what the narrator interjects, or interrupts, to tell the **MARK THE TEXT** girls. Why do you think she reminds them about this?

_____

_____

_____

Reading Strategy: Recognizing Cause and Effect Relationships

Why does the counselor feel relieved? Underline the sentence that answers this **MARK THE TEXT** question. Why must the bunk feel safe?

_____

_____

_____

Almost before Adar could finish her question, Aman was ready to answer. Aman is a strong, athletic Palestinian who does not waste her words. When she begins to speak, she is both **intimidating** and impressive as she defends her opinions.

Calm and **composed**, she explained to Adar that the presence of Muslim holy sites in Jerusalem meant that the Palestinians were the rightful **proprietors** of the city. With an equally rapid response, Adar reminded her that Jerusalem also contained Jewish holy sites.

Aman seems prepared for this answer. "We would be very nice to you [the Jewish people]. We would always let you come visit your sites, just like all the other tourists," she replied.

Adar had no intention of allowing her people to become theoretical tourists in this debate: "Well, we have the city now," Adar said. "You can't just make us leave, because it's ours. We might decide to give some of it to the Palestinians, but it belongs to us now."

I spent such times in the bunk listening. I only **sporadically** interjected my voice, reminding them not to hold each other, as individuals, responsible for the actions of their governments.

The conversation eventually wound down. As the girls drifted off to sleep, I felt relieved. As much as I want the girls in my bunk to express all their concerns and thoughts, any conversation about such a sensitive issue keeps me tense. The bunk must feel safe but issues of conflict can't be ignored or downplayed. As a bunk counselor, I must provide campers with the safety and security they need to continue the process of breaking down barriers.

---

intimidating, threatening or scary
composed, thoughtful
proprietors, owners
sporadically, from time to time

Retell It!

Retell the article from the point of view of one of the campers.

_____

_____

_____

_____

_____

_____

_____

_____

_____

Reader's Response

What new insights did this article give you about the Mideast conflict or about war and peace in general?

_____

_____

_____

_____

_____

_____

_____

_____

Think About the Skill

How did identifying problems and solutions help you better understand the article?

_____

_____

_____

GRAMMAR

Use with textbook page 262.

Compound and Complex Sentences

Writing is more interesting when a writer uses a variety of different sentence types. The paragraph below is less interesting than it could be. It uses only **simple sentences**.

> I liked summer camp. Many of the kids were from around here. A few were from other towns. The food was delicious. I looked forward to meals. The treasure hunts were held in a huge forest. These were the best activities. I found a compass. I'm going to give it to my sister.

To add variety, a writer can do the following:

- Make **compound sentences** by combining **simple sentences** using *and, but, yet, for, nor, or,* or *so*:

  Many of the kids were from around here, **but** a few were from other towns. The food was delicious, **so** I looked forward to meals.

- Make **complex sentences** by using the relative pronouns *that, which,* and *who:*

  The treasure hunts, **which** were held in a huge forest, were the best activities. I'm going to give the compass **that** I found to my sister.

Write *S* for simple, *C* for compound, or *CX* for complex next to each sentence.

Example: ___C___ I liked one girl very much, and we are still friends.

1. _____ Jim shared a cabin with Jason.

2. _____ They had very different opinions, so they argued all the time.

3. _____ Jim's counselor said that Jim argued with other campers, too.

4. _____ Jason wanted to change cabins, but the counselor wouldn't let him.

5. _____ After a week, which wasn't a pleasant one, Jim and Jason learned to get along.

GRAMMAR

Use after the lesson on using the simple future.

Using the Simple Future
Use the **simple future** tense to describe an event that will take place in the future. There are two forms of the simple future, a form of *be* + *going to* + verb or *will* + verb.

Rewrite each sentence twice, using two forms of the simple future tense.
Example: I work in a school.

I am going to work in a school.   *I will work in a school.*

1. I teach at the camp.

_____   _____

2. We discuss politics.

_____   _____

3. They sing songs.

_____   _____

4. You read this article.

_____   _____

5. It rains.

_____   _____

Rewrite each sentence, changing the verb in parentheses ( ) to the simple future.

6. Camp (begin) very soon.

_____

7. The campers (arrive) next Thursday.

_____

8. Adar (sleep) in a bunk bed.

_____

9. They (learn) about one another's homes.

_____

10. Most campers (enjoy) their summer.

_____

SKILLS FOR WRITING

Use with textbook page 263.

Focusing on Paragraph Unity

A **paragraph** has **unity** when all of the sentences support or tell about the topic sentence. Paragraph unity makes a paragraph easier to read because it helps the reader follow and understand the ideas.

Read the following paragraph. Then answer the questions about it.

> My cousin David doesn't let barriers get in his way. Although he is sight-impaired, he can do anything. David reads Braille and attends a regular high school. He loves to read about Helen Keller. He is a member of the debate team and is an honor student. He dislikes going to the dentist. David also loves sports and is a member of the track team. In fact, he is a long-distance runner. He is also one of the school's best sprinters. He gets energy by eating our grandmother's apple pie after school. He also shares a room with his brother, Billy. Last year, David was chosen the best student of the year.

1. Who is the paragraph about?

_____

_____

2. What is the main idea of the paragraph? _____

_____

3. Which details support the main idea? _____

_____

_____

4. Which details do not belong in the paragraph? _____

_____

5. Choose one of the details that does not belong in this paragraph. Tell why it does

not belong. _____

_____

PROOFREADING AND EDITING

Use with textbook page 264.

Read the story below carefully. Find the mistakes. Then rewrite the story correctly on the lines below.

This summer i read *The Story of My Life* by Helen Keller. The experience change my own life. Before I read Helen Kellers story, I often felt sorry for myself. I looked at small problems as huge barriers Sometimes I was jealous of student who were good athletes. I wished I could be as strong and fast as they were. I was also jealous of students who did their homework much fast than I do. My homework always take me a while.

After I read the book, everything changed. I thought Helen Keller's story was amazeing. She overcame so many serious difficultys. Now I realize that any problem can be overcome, so I dont have to be jealous of others.

_____

_____

_____

_____

_____

_____

_____

_____

_____

_____

_____

_____

_____

_____

SPELLING

Use after the spelling lesson.

Spelling Schwa Sounds

A **schwa** sound is the sound of the vowel in an unaccented syllable. It can be represented by each of the vowels.

> *a*: about, attempts, realize
> *e*: happen, fragments, marvel
> *i*: imitate, indicate, robin
> *o*: second, weapon, contain
> *u*: circus, medium, focus

Look at the words in the box. Say each word aloud. Listen for the schwa sound. Then write the words in the chart under the letter that represents its schwa sound.

agree	towel	pencil	author	awful
attend	autumn	family	broken	blossom

Schwa sound spelled with *a*	Schwa sound spelled with *e*	Schwa sound spelled with *i*	Schwa sound spelled with *o*	Schwa sound spelled with *u*
1.	3.	5.	7.	9.
2.	4.	6.	8.	10.

ACKNOWLEDGMENTS

American Camping Association, Inc. "Understanding Cultural Differences" by Sandy Cameron, reprinted from *Camping Magazine* by permission of the American Camping Association, Inc. Copyright © by the American Camping Association, Inc.

Arte Público Press—University of Houston. "Mirror, Mirror: Mambo No. 5" by Gustavo Pérez Firmat is reprinted with permission from the publisher of *Little Havana Blues: A Cuban-American Literary Anthology* (Houston: Arte Público Press—University of Houston, Copyright © 1996).

Brandt & Hochman Literary Agents, Inc. "Nancy Hanks" by Rosemary Carr and Stephen Vincent Benét. From *A Book of Americans* by Rosemary and Stephen Vincent Benét, copyright © 1933 by Rosemary and Stephen Vincent Benét. Copyright renewed © 1961 by Rosemary and Stephen Vincent Benét. Reprinted by permission of Brandt & Hochman Literary Agents, Inc.

Rita Dove. "Lady Freedom Among Us" from *On the Bus with Rosa Parks*, W.W. Norton, © 1999 by Rita Dove. Reprinted by permission of the author.

Martha Staid. "On van Gogh's *Starry Night*" by Martha Staid. Reprinted by permission of the author.

Mandy Terc. "Sowing the Seeds of Peace" by Mandy Terc. In memory of the founder of Seeds of Peace, John Wallach, for his vision and the campers of Seeds of Peace, for their courage. Reprinted by permission of the author.